You Can't Win

Also by Howard Burman

A Story Told by Two Liars
A Man Called Shoeless
Willie, Mickey & The Duke
Paradise by Paradise
Here Be Dragons
Gentlemen At The Bat

You Can't Win

✦

One Woman's Struggle With the Casinos

Barbara Zajak with Howard Burman

iUniverse, Inc.
New York   Bloomington

You Can't Win
One Woman's Struggle With the Casinos

iUniverse books may be ordered through booksellers or by contacting:

iUniverse
1663 Liberty Drive
Bloomington, IN 47403
www.iuniverse.com
1-800-Authors (1-800-288-4677)

Because of the dynamic nature of the Internet, any Web addresses or links contained
in this book may have changed since publication and may no longer be valid.

ISBN: 978-1-4502-0449-1 (sc)
ISBN: 978-1-4502-0450-7 (ebk)

Printed in the United States of America

iUniverse rev. date: 1/19/2010

To John:

Our marriage is stronger now because of your will to see our marriage through a bad situation. You never gave up on me when I thought I wasn't worth fighting for. Our love for each other can withstand anything because of you. Please realize how much I love you and respect you. I'll always remember that without you I could not have had the courage and strength to write our story. With all my love, your wife "forever".

To Denise:

Thank you for all the wonderful years as being best friends. You have been there for me through the toughest times in my life. Our friendship of over 30 years is a true blessing. You were my rock when I couldn't see through my emotional roller coaster. I love you with all my heart and I am so thankful for our true friendship.

To Mickey:

You are a wonderful person. Thank you for all your understanding and compassion. You have always showed me unconditional love as you do with your whole family and I am blessed to have you as a mother-in-law. Your words of wisdom and showing me how to turn bad situations into a positive learning experience have inspired me. I will always cherish our relationship.

To Judge Gregory Bill:

Without your encourqagement this book would never have been written.

To Howard:

Without you my life story would just be personal notes. You are a very generous, caring person. There are no words I can say to express my appreciation. Thank you from the bottom of my heart.

--Barbara

Author's Note

This is a true story. However, some of the names in this book have been changed in order to maintain the dignity and privacy of others.

December 9, 2006, Detroit, Michigan

I already have the lie figured out. If John calls I'll tell him I'm shopping. Christmas is only two weeks away. It's a reasonable story. He'll believe that. I drive to the MGM Grand Casino trying to fight off the guilt. The instant I walk through the inviting doors of MGM's Technicolor world I feel a pulse of excitement wash over me. It's 12:30 in the afternoon and already the place is buzzing. I try a few machines but I'm constantly checking my cell phone to see if John has called. The room is noisy enough that I could easily miss the ring. After every few plays I reach into my purse for the phone. Nothing. I know he'll call, though. He'll be checking for sure. "I'm looking for a scarf for your mother," I'll say. When I get home without one I'll tell him I couldn't find one I thought she'd like. "Do you think blue or brown is better?" I've gotten real good with the lies.

I'm on a machine I've never played before so I'm not quite sure what to expect.

I take a deep breath and reach for my Newport Menthol 100's while I sip my usual drink—Diet Pepsi with three cherries.

I'm feeling lucky because my left hand is itching. Always a good sign.

I start playing triple sevens, a dollar machine. I'm playing $3 per spin, the max.

I plug in a few dollar coins, push the button, check the phone. A few more dollars drop. I'm looking for a red, a white, and a blue seven for a big payoff. The magic wheels spin in a blur. The first 7 comes up red, the next a triple sign, then another triple sign. My heart starts pounding. I know what this means. Two triple signs and a red 7 pays 9 times the amount on the pay table.

The glorious, wonderful, fantastic, stunning sound of bells and flashing lights. For a brief moment I freeze. The fat lady at the next machine looks over at me with that look of jealousy I know well. I don't know exactly what the payoff is, but those bells tell me it's good.

I'm on a main walkway so lots of people come over to look. This is one of the reasons people spend time here. A big winner!

If John calls now, the bells will give me away. I won't answer but

I'll call him back in a few minutes and tell him I had my hands full and couldn't get to the phone just then.

I am grinning the grin of a happy gambler. "Way to go," someone says over my shoulder.

How many times have I pushed these buttons without winning? I can't even imagine. Now comes the big payoff. I'm a big winner. Finally!

The bells bring not only some onlookers, but also a burly man from the casino.

"Congratulations" he says in a dull tone.

"Thank you," *I say as if I've just done something more important than pushing a button.*

"Can I see your driver's license?" he says.

Instantly the exhilaration turns to fear and I begin shaking. I reach into my purse for my wallet and see the phone. No, I wish John were here. I don't like this at all. I have some difficulty sliding my license out from the plastic envelope because of the shakes. I know the man can see this.

"And your social security card," *he adds.*

While I'm digging for the card several security guards come and surround me. I hand over the license and card. The man looks at them for a moment. As much as I try, I can't stop shaking.

He puts the cards in his jacket pocket. "Would you mind coming with us, please," *he says very pleasantly so as not to alarm the ever-growing crowd of onlookers.*

Escorted by an undercover officer and a uniformed guard, we make our way through aisles of familiar machines to a private elevator off to the side of the cashier' cages. No one says anything to me. I am scared beyond belief. All I can think about is John. I don't want him to know, but at the same time I want him to tell me what to do. Oh, my God, I think, what if they take my phone and he calls!

A female guard is in the elevator.

"Put your hands out to your sides" *she says as she pats me down.* "We have to make sure you don't have any weapons on you."

"Weapons?"

"Just a precaution."

I don't know if we're going up or down. I'm too scared to notice, but shortly the doors slide open and I'm led to a small room with a table and some chairs--just like in the movies. I'm told to sit.

I'm in serious trouble and I know it. I start to cry.

ONE

✦

It's the order of things. First a little lie, then a bigger one, and soon it becomes who you are.

I can't remember when I first noticed the change. I can't say I didn't see it coming. I just didn't want to believe it. I guess that isn't much of an excuse, but it's the truth. If I had been able to look years into the future and see myself as the lying, tormented person I became, I never would have recognized myself.

This was before the lies. Before the slots. Before Bobby and John.

I grew up in a Detroit suburb as one of nine children in a strict Catholic family. I was the second oldest of six girls and I had three younger brothers. By the time my parents stopped having babies, we all crowded into a little brown three bedroom house just like all the other little brown houses in the neighborhood. My parents had one bedroom, the boys one, and all six of us girls crammed in another. Since birth control was off limits in this mostly Catholic neighborhood, there were kids running all over the place.

Although religion wasn't discussed around the house very much, we were made to go to church every Sunday and despite the fact that money was always an issue for us, we were all sent to St. Agatha, a private Catholic school. Father, it seemed, could always come up with enough money for the two things he cared most about—Catholic school and alcohol.

My first day at St. Agatha's was, to say the least, traumatic. All that summer I had been dreading the thought of leaving my mother. She escorted me to the classroom, told me everything was going to be okay and went home. I was so terrified that, in front of the other children and the nun who was our teacher, I wet my pants. The nun looked at me like I had just committed a mortal sin against God and the Church, grabbed me by the arm and marched me into the front office where she called my mother to come and take me home. My mother was ashamed, I was embarrassed, my father was furious.

The next day I was again marched to school where I had to face the other children and the teacher again. I managed to control myself although I knew everyone thought there was something wrong with me, and they were right. I was extremely self-conscious and shy. Throughout my school days I did everything I could not to draw attention to myself. If I could have made myself invisible, I would have.

I suppose it's sad really, but the only good memory I have of kindergarten is the Easter parade where we all walked down the aisle with our Easter bonnets, singing songs, and looking for our moms.

Kindergarten was bad enough, but first grade was a total nightmare. Although I did everything I could to avoid notice, our teacher, a very stern nun, singled me out because I was left-handed. She believed it was unnatural to write that way. Something must be seriously wrong with this timid young girl. I always tried to write with my right hand, but sometimes I would forget and pick up the pencil with the "wrong" hand. If she saw me, and it seems like she had eyes in the back of her head, she would storm down the aisle and smack my hand with a wicked pointer stick and then make me stand in the little dark closet at the back of the room. It didn't take much of an imagination to know what the other kids were thinking.

One day I came home with a particularly red and puffy hand as the result of an especially vicious whack. Mom took one look at the hand and asked what happened. I told her how I was always being punished because I was wrong-handed. Well, Mom wouldn't have it, so she immediately went to the school to confront the torturer nun. I don't know what she said, but I do know from that day on, I was never hit again.

I've since learned that left-handed people are actually supposed to be smarter, but it never seemed that way to me despite that people like

Albert Einstein and Benjamin Franklin were left-handed. I always had this feeling that I was labeled dumb, and did the nuns ever make sure I felt that way!

The fact is though, school was hard for me and I struggled just to get decent grades. No matter how much I studied I couldn't get the grades that Maura, my older sister, got even though she hardly studied at all. The only thing I was even reasonably good at was spelling because I could memorize the lists of words. When it came time for grades to be passed out I was even more nervous than usual. The priest would come to each classroom to pass out the report cards. He'd call out the names of each student, and one by one we had to go stand in front of the class while he made comments about our grades. When he called my name I just wanted to die and be done with it because he always had something negative to say.

"Barbara, now you know these aren't very good. What's wrong, darling? I know you can do better."

If that wasn't bad enough, I then had to take the cards home and face my parents. Mom understood I was trying, but my father would just scowl and say, "You're grounded." He never offered encouragement, never showed sympathy.

I didn't have any friends at grade school. I always thought it was because of my looks. I was very tall for my age, and very, very skinny. I never fit in with any group so it was easier for me just to stay quiet and unnoticed. The last thing in the world I ever wanted to do was make waves and draw attention to myself.

The only friends I did have were a few neighbor kids, but they went to public school, so I didn't see them a lot.

I suppose every neighborhood has a bully. Ours was a nasty boy named Chuckie Prebie. One day walking home from school, he sneaked up behind me and pushed me down hard on the sidewalk. I lay there bleeding and crying until Mom rescued me and took me home to clean my wounds.

When Dad came home and heard what happened, he sent my oldest brother, after Chuckie. My brother, Mark, eventually caught up with Chuckie and held him in a choke hold until he turned blue. Dad beamed with pride at hearing the news. I can't honestly remember him beaming with pride at anything I ever did.

A few years later Chuckie moved away and I heard he was killed.

I was always very sensitive about my tall, skinny looks and other kids often made fun of me. Most of the time I just went out of my way to avoid them, but one day, for some reason, the kid sitting behind me in class made a another rude comment that really got to me.

"Hey, Olive Oyl, I hear Bluto's coming after you" he said.

In those days everyone knew Olive Oyl as the character in the Popeye cartoons. She was tall and skinny like me, with short hair and enormous feet. Bluto was the character who was always kidnapping her.

When this kid called me Olive Oyl I ran out of the class as fast as I could and raced straight to the office. The secretary told me I had to go back to class, but I told her to call Mom to come and get me which she eventually did.

On the way home, Mom asked me what happened and I told her I was fed up with being teased all the time because of my looks.

All she said was, "Kids are mean. They don't understand how much they are hurting you."

This was just another situation of a male figure in my life showing me I wasn't worth anything.

Even as a young girl, much of the work in the house fell to me, but that was okay because as long as I did everything Mom asked me to do, I could go unnoticed and life was a little bit easier. So I concentrated on helping out Mom with the house cleaning, the cooking, and taking care of the younger kids. My parents didn't seem to mind that Maura had little interest in helping around the house and so she contributed little. I, though, had a natural maternal instinct, and taking care of the younger ones came easy to me.

When Mom was in the hospital giving birth to my seven younger siblings, I had to take care of everything around the house. When I was seven, she went in again to have surgery on her thyroid, so Maura and I had to take turns staying home from school and taking care of the younger kids. Even then, Maura did as little as she possibly could get away with and I ended up doing the lion's share. My grandmother, who lived close, could have come in and taken care of things, but she was a beer drinker, and despite the fact that so was Dad, Mom didn't want her staying at the house.

I guess it was because I had so many problems with my father that I became much closer with my mother. Still, she was a stern woman and not very loving. She didn't take much care of her physical appearance and never went to the dentist which resulted in rotting teeth. The only times I can remember her dressing up, taking care with her makeup, and spending any time at all fixing her dark short hair were on the very rare occurrences when she and Dad were going out.

I think it's fair to say she was an unhappy woman who, because she was a good Catholic, had more children then she would have liked. Oh, she could get angry with Father at times, but there was a strict limit to how far she would go. Father always had the final word.

My parents grew up in the same neighborhood but didn't have the same group of friends. Dad was known to be something of a lady's man. Mother was a good girl who focused on school.

When Dad was 18 he was drafted into the army. When he returned a few years later, he ran into Mom in a bar where her parents had taken her to celebrate her 21st birthday. He asked her to dance and shortly after that they began dating. My grandparents didn't approve because they remembered his younger wild ways. Despite this, they got married and eventually my grandparents came to accept him.

Father was not happy with me. I know that because he made it very clear, and so I always tip-toed around him so as not to make him upset. He could be extremely verbally abusive, and the disgust in his eyes when he looked at me was impossible to miss. I can honestly say I felt as if he didn't want me anywhere around. He seemed to have a real problem with the fact that unlike the other kids I was tall and scrawny. I stood out. I looked different and, for whatever reason, he hated that. This wasn't something you could discuss with him so I never dared bring it up.

He was a good-looking man, tall, dark-haired and muscular. He started out in the heating and cooling business and then went on to become an electrician. Like Mother, though, over time he let his appearance go. I think the heavy drinking and smoking took its toll.

Every day after work he'd stop at the Lucky Seven Bar before coming home. Sometimes it would be beer, sometimes liquor, sometimes both. More than once I can remember Mother piling all us kids in the station wagon in our pjs and driving to the bar to see if his work truck was still there—and it always was.

If we did something to upset Mom, when Dad came home he would line up the four oldest in the basement and beat us with his belt. It didn't seem to matter who the culprit was, all four of us got the beating. Standing there in the line waiting for the lashes, I'd always wet my pants.

Once I turned the TV on without realizing he was sleeping. Apparently he was drunk and woke up in a rage. I managed to get away from him and ran to my bedroom, threw myself on my bed, and covered my head with a pillow. He stormed in and began flogging me with his belt and then punching me all over my body with his fists. My screams and crying brought Mom who finally got him to stop. When I went into the bathroom to clean myself up I could see that my left eye was bloodshot and swollen and I had red welts all over my body. Mom was furious with Dad but I know what both of them were thinking. I had to go to school the next day and there would be questions about what happened to my eye.

For the first time in my life I got up the courage to stand up to Dad.

"If you ever land a hand on me again, I'll call the police," I said.

I looked him straight in the eye and could see that he knew I was serious.

I think Mom was afraid something else was going to happen. "Go to your room," she said to me.

Of course, as usual, I did as I was told. For the rest of the night I stayed in my room, but I was proud that I had stood up to him, and as far as I know, that was the last time he ever laid hands on any of us. Still, to this day the inside of my eye shows signs of the beating, a constant reminder of Father's drunken rages.

On Maura's 13th birthday, Dad came home with a big, beautifully wrapped box for her. She was so elated when she ripped it open and found a lovely pink dress, she smiled from ear to ear and I was so happy for her.

When my 13th birthday was nearing I was so excited for days that I could hardly sleep. The thought of a beautiful new dress filled me with great joy.

When the day came I patiently waited all afternoon for Dad to come home with the present. I waited a long time because he didn't show up until late in the evening. I peeked through the curtains when I heard his truck pull up. He was empty-handed. Perhaps he has it hidden in the house I thought. He came in slightly drunk and went to bed.

I was so devastated I cried myself to sleep and learned it was better not to expect too much from life. That way there would be fewer disappointments.

Because there were eleven of us crammed into the small house, Father, who was always good with his hands, built a wall in the basement so that four of us could sleep down there. One side was for Maura and me and the other for my two oldest brothers. Since there were no doors to the rooms, Mom sewed curtains to hang on rods.

My oldest brother, Mark had always been a real trouble maker. Nevertheless, he was the apple of Father's eye and could do no wrong. Named after Father, he was next in age to me.

One evening when I was in my early teens he came into my room where I was lying on the bed in my pajamas reading a book for school. I don't know where Maura was, but she wasn't there. I thought Mark was going to ask me a question but he just stood there staring at me.

"Get out of here," I said.

Acting like a tough guy he said, "Take your clothes off."

"Are you crazy? Get out of here."

"I said, take your clothes off."

"Don't be a jerk. Leave me alone," I said getting off the bed. I didn't know what to think, but I never trusted Mark.

He immediately shoved me backwards down onto the bed and began pulling my bottoms off. I started kicking and screaming but there was no one else in the basement and upstairs you couldn't hear anything from down there. I was trying to kick him away from me but he was much stronger and in a few moments he had my bottoms completely off. I was scared stiff as he slid his pants down around his ankles.

I kept struggling as he began breathing harder and harder and then ejaculated without actually raping me.

He got off of me yanking his pants up.

"Say anything about this and I'll kill you. Do you understand?"

I didn't say anything. I didn't have to. The look on my face said it all.

"One word and you're dead."

As he turned to leave the room, I threw the little table lamp at him but missed. He turned, snickered, and then walked away.

Whether he would have carried through on his threat I don't know, but I was frightened enough of him that I didn't say anything to anyone. I should have, I know, but I didn't. I certainly wasn't going to tell Father.

This went on for another six months. I did everything I could to avoid being in the basement if he were there. It was a small house so it was difficult to find space to get away from him. Sometimes I would find excuses to sleep in one of the upstairs bedrooms with one of my younger sisters. Whenever my parents were gone, he did everything he could to corner me.

There was a time when I was taking a shower downstairs and he just opened the shower door and started fondling me, I fought back but he could overpower me in an instant. I was all of 110 pounds and was 5' 8." Several times he burst into my bedroom at night and jumped on top of me, pulling my clothes off and ejaculating. I knew better than to scream because I knew his temper and I knew how brutal he could be. I was simply terrified.

When some years later I heard that he actually raped one of my younger sisters, I was filled with guilt which I carried around for a long time. I felt it was my fault because it might not have happened had I told someone.

Maybe my sexual inhibitions and problems with the opposite sex started here, or maybe this just made them worse. Anyway, a pattern of sexual abuse had begun.

When I was fifteen I heard about a job opening at Herc's Beef Buffet, a local restaurant. I thought working part-time there would get me out of the house and away from Mark and my father for at least a few more hours each week. Mother was dead set against it, but Father was happy any time he didn't have to look at me, so after some haggling and then finally agreeing that the money I brought home would be very helpful in a household that always needed it, I took the job.

From the first day I loved working there. It gave me a sense of independence, of freedom from the tensions at home, and a chance to do something well. Right away I showed a good work ethic and I think the Hercs really appreciated that. It felt wonderful to be told you were good at something and I know the money came in handy.

The restaurant was a very popular and usually a very busy place and I liked to be kept busy. It was in a large brick building with a big dining area and a fireplace. The main attraction was the beef round that was carved to the customer's liking, but there was also turkey, spaghetti and meatballs, fish of the day, as well as pies, desserts, and drinks. My job was to work behind a steam table in the main dish area. Even though I was so young, I was put there because I was tall enough to be able to serve the main dish over the steam table. For once, my height was an advantage.

For the first few months, everything was fine—the owners liked me, and I liked the job.

Then I started having problems with a man who worked there. He was married to a daughter of the Hercs. It seems that no matter how hard I tried, I couldn't get away from men with drinking problems.

It began when one day he came up behind me while I was at the steam table and grabbed my buttocks. He thought it was funny, but I jumped away angry and humiliated.

"Don't," was about all I could manage to get out.

He winked and walked away.

I thought that was the end of it, but it was actually just the beginning. Every chance he got to corner me, he would touch and fondle me in inappropriate places. When I had to go back to the cooler he would follow and fondle me. I always pushed him away and let him know in no uncertain terms that I didn't want him to do it again. I did everything I could to stay clear of him, especially when he was drinking. Nothing I did stopped him, though. He followed and fondled me every time he could get away with it.

I didn't want to make a scene, but I know everyone in the restaurant knew what he was doing, including his wife, but no one said anything to him or to me. It was as if everyone was saying it's perfectly all right to sexually abuse a young girl. Looking the other way was better than stepping in to stop it.

As much as I liked my job, I never thought about quitting or telling my parents. Like so much else in my life, I just bottled it up. Besides, I figured if I told my father he would just blame me.

Eventually Mrs. Herc, who I think knew exactly what was going on, let me change shifts so that I didn't have to work at the same time as my tormentor. Still, for a long time I got skittery anytime someone came up behind me.

It was yet another episode leading to my growing distrust of men.

Father was constantly making snide comments about how I looked and how I dressed. Don't ask me why, but in terms of family looks, I was really the odd one out. All the other kids were of average height and a little on the heavy side. I was anything but. Father acted like he not only thought that was bad, but that it was my fault. It was almost like, "How dare you stick out like that." He had very definite ideas about how young girls should dress and let me know at every opportunity that I was letting him down. My problem was that just about everything I wore was too short for me, including my school uniform.

"You're not leaving the house dressed like that," he'd say.

But I didn't have any choice. I couldn't find a pair of pants that were long enough for me so I was always wearing dresses, skirts, or shorts, and he thought that made me look "easy."

"You know what kind of men you're going to attract dressing like that?" he was always saying.

Over and over again Mom stepped in and tried to explain that she couldn't find pants that were long enough for my thin frame. I don't know, maybe if we had more money we could have gone to a special store or something, but where we shopped we couldn't find nice looking clothing for me.

When I was going to meet some of the girls from Herc's he'd say something like, "Who you going to meet tonight, some gigolo?"

It never stopped.

One day, when my parents got it into their minds that they would like to have a picture taken of all nine children, they called a local photographer who came over to the house for the sitting. He took a lot of time getting all of the squirming kids into the positions he wanted and finally managed to take the pictures.

When he was packing his gear back up, he told my parents that the proofs would be available in a few days, and then added, "You know, you should consider getting your daughter there into modeling." He was looking at me. "She might do well. I mean she's got the looks for a model—tall, slender. That's the type they want these days."

I always thought that models had to be pretty and I never considered myself that, because I never had any boys interested in me. I wasn't "tall and slender," I was a gangly ugly duckling.

"Sure," the photographer went on. "I know some people in the business. You know, as a photographer I've shot a lot of young ladies like her."

"Well, I never thought of that," said Mother.

"Let me make a few enquiries on her behalf," he said as he was going out the door. "I'll try to set something up. You know, an audition."

At this point, Father who had been glaring at me like I had done something horrendous, said, "No thank you. We're not interested."

"Well, just give it some thought," said the photographer.

"I said we're not interested," Father snapped. "Good bye."

A few days later, when the photographer returned with the proofs, he brought up the idea again.

Father would have none of it. "My daughter is not a slut," he said practically yelling in the poor man's face. "Models are all sluts. I don't want you bring it up again."

Even though I didn't think I could ever be a model, I would like to have had the opportunity to find out about it, but when Father said no, that was it.

After that, I dressed even more plainly than ever. I didn't need any more of Father's disgusted looks.

Father came down with colon cancer when he was only 45. They had to take out a large portion of his colon. He was in the hospital for several weeks and then came home to recuperate, so for several months he was off work. Money which was tight enough during normal times became even more of a problem. We quickly went through whatever savings there were and I didn't have any problem giving some of my weekly paycheck from the restaurant to Mom for groceries. Maura, who was also working at the time and had been given a used car by

Dad, refused to help out at all. She needed the money herself she insisted. She was, if nothing else, a selfish person.

If I gave her gas money she'd drive me to work so at least there was some advantage to me.

When I was old enough to start driving I practiced a little in Maura's car, making sure I'd paid for the gas, and then Mom took me for the driving test. When I got to the DMV, a nice man with a cheery face sat on the passenger's side and told me what he wanted me to do. Well, I was so nervous, and screwed up so badly that he quickly ended the test.

"You're going to have to practice some more and then reschedule," he said as he climbed out of the car. "Your mother can drive you home."

I was so absolutely mortified that I told Mom I was never going to take the test again. I didn't need to drive anyway.

"You were just a little nervous," Mom said. "You'll do better next time."

"There isn't going to be a next time."

"You'll change your mind. Every teenager wants to drive."

"I'm not going to go through that again."

"We'll see."

Of course I really wanted to drive. I just didn't want to be embarrassed again. Eventually I got up the courage to try again. This time I passed—barely.

Father didn't buy me a car as he did Maura when she passed her test, but by now, I didn't expect to get the same treatment as her anyway. I had learned different.

Maura usually got good grades but once when she came home with an unusually poor report card, Father took the car keys away from her. Naturally he did not give them to me. The result was that she had to quit her job while I took the bus to the restaurant.

After I graduated from high school, I was able to buy my parents' old station wagon with money I had saved and graduation money and so, despite my annoyance with Maura, I began going to bars with her on the weekends where we'd have a few beers. She offered me a chance to get out of the house for a while and I took it. She was 18 and I could usually slide by bouncers unnoticed. Usually we'd go to a place called

Uncle Sam's, a bar where Canadian men would come across the river to meet girls. It was always crowded so I felt like I could blend into the crowd and not be noticed.

One night Maura met Jeff, one of the Canadians, and really a nice guy. She tried to fix me up with some of his friends but none of them were interested in me. That was okay because I was only there anyway to escape from the situation at home.

Naturally we had a curfew which Maura managed to get set at 1:00 A.M. One Friday night as we were leaving, she said, "Let's stop and get something to eat. I'm starved."

"We'll be late," I said.

"So what? They'll be asleep. I mean it's not like we don't know how to sneak in."

"Speak for yourself."

"Come on, I'll show you."

We did stop and get some early breakfast so it wasn't until close to 3:00 A.M. when we got home. We parked down the street so the car wouldn't wake anybody and then slipped around to the back door.

"I'll go in and make sure the coast is clear," she whispered. "I know how to do this. Wait a minute and then follow me."

She went in and when I didn't hear anything for a few moments, I followed. Maura had made it safely into the bedroom unnoticed, but I didn't get three steps into the house when Father appeared in front of me.

"You little sneaking slut," he said. "I told you 1:00 o'clock, didn't I? Didn't I?"

"Yes."

"It's now 3:00 o'clock, isn't it?"

"Yes."

"What the fuck is wrong with you?"

He then proceeded to call me every name you could possibly imagine. He could swear up a storm when he got angry, but never "goddamnit." Mother wouldn't allow that.

I was so worried about what Dad was going to do that I didn't sleep much all night.

"Don't worry about it," Maura said. "You worry too much."

"You know Dad."

"Look, he'll be over it by morning."

He wasn't. The next day he told me to get my things together and move out of the house.

"If you can't be trusted, I don't want you living in this house, and you obviously can't be trusted. Get the hell out."

I looked at Mother and knew she wanted to step in and stop this, but when Father got into one of these angry moods, there was no denying him.

The longer I stood there not saying anything, the more furious he became, but at times like this talking back made a bad situation even worse.

"You want to live by your rules, then go do it on your own you sneaky bitch."

He had to know Maura was with me, but he didn't say a word about her and I certainly wasn't going to bring her into this.

"Be gone by tonight," he ordered as he was leaving the room. You ain't staying here, that's for damn sure."

I had expected him to be angry, but I never expected this. All of a sudden I was alone and had no plans. Where was I going to go? I didn't make a lot of money at Herc's and buying the station wagon had taken all of my savings. Instantly I panicked.

For the first few nights I stayed in some local motels but then Nicky, a friend from Herc's, told me her parents were away on vacation and that if I wanted, I could stay with her for a couple of weeks. The motel was taking a lot of what I was earning, so I agreed. I wasn't sure what I was going to do in the long run, but at least that would give me some time to figure things out.

On the day after I moved in with her, we decided to go to a shopping mall that was some distance from her house. After driving for a while, she realized she had forgotten her purse so we made a quick U turn and were heading back to her house in her little blue Datsun going about 50 miles an hour when a large black car suddenly swerved across the center yellow lines and hit us head-on. I was knocked out cold.

I woke up as a man was pounding on my window.

"Are you okay?"

"I was so groggy I couldn't even answer."

"Don't worry, help is on the way."

Nicky apparently never lost consciousness and was screaming but through my semi-conscious fog she sounded as if she were a mile away.

We were outside of the city a ways, so it took some time for the police to arrive.

"Can you get out?" an officer asked me.

"I can't," I said.

I don't really remember a lot of what happened next except that they managed to get me out and onto a stretcher and then into an ambulance. Nicky was already sitting in it crying. It was a long drive back to a hospital. I was still so groggy that all I could think of was to call out for Mom.

"We phoned her," I heard a voice say. "She'll be at the hospital when we get there."

I started crying.

"Try to stay calm. You'll be okay."

When they were taking me out of the ambulance I saw Mom and my brother Mark standing there looking very worried.

They wheeled me into the emergency room asking me questions about what hurt and where I felt anything strange, but I was crying so much I really couldn't answer. Then they started talking to Mom about me but I couldn't understand anything they were saying. Everything was a blur. A doctor examined me but didn't say anything to me which frightened me even more.

They left me in a room for a while. Eventually Mother came in.

"You'll be okay, honey," she said. "Laid up for a little while but okay."

"What did they say? What's wrong?"

"Just a nasty concussion and whiplash. Oh, and badly bruised ribs and your left leg. It's not broken or anything, but I think you'll need crutches for a while."

I thought there was something she wasn't telling me. "What else?"

"That's it. You were very lucky. You might have been killed. Very lucky."

I certainly didn't feel lucky but I guess I really was. Later, my brother helped me out of the bed and a nurse came in and showed me how to use the crutches.

As we were driving away from the hospital, Mom said Father

agreed that I could return home for a couple of weeks while I was healing. Still, when we got to the house, I could see him glaring out the front window and I could tell by the look on his face that he was not happy about my being back. I knew the look well.

I wasn't surprised when the minute we were in the door he said, "As soon as you're better, you're out of here."

All of my brothers and sisters were there, looking at me like I was some creature from Mars. When I managed to navigate myself into the bathroom on the crutches and looked into the mirror, I almost fainted. The left side of my face was swollen and as red as a beet and my eye was almost completely closed.

When I asked about Nicky, Mom said she also bruised ribs and whiplash but wasn't as bad off as I was.

That night I slept with Debbie, my youngest sister. I guess I was scared all night because she told me I tossed and turned with bad dreams and wet the bed.

Once again I was terribly embarrassed.

I tried my darndest to stay clear of Father and to do everything I could to help Mom while still hobbling around on crutches. By the second week Dad was clearly getting impatient that I was still there. He was never hard to read about such things, so I talked with Mom about asking Dad if I could stay. I knew I couldn't ask him, but I thought she could. I wasn't crazy about the idea but I had been off work for a few weeks because of the accident and so I was short of money, and I knew Nicky's parents were back so returning there wasn't an option. She said she'd bring up the subject when the time was right. Eventually she did and despite his reluctance, she got Father to agree just so long as I paid rent.

So for better or worse, I was back home.

It wasn't long before Maura moved out of the house and into a trailer park and it wasn't long before she got into trouble. One day I got a frantic call from Mother telling me Maura had been arrested for passing bad checks. I got off work early and drove Mom to the jail where she had to make good on the checks. She then launched into a long lecture to Maura about taking responsibility. Maura nodded in agreement but I knew there was a lot going on in her life that my parents didn't know about. Among other things, she was planning on moving across the river to Canada where she would be living with Jeff. Of course, she told my parents that she would be living alone in her own apartment. What else could she say? Father would have gone completely ballistic if he knew she was living with a boy before she was married. Mom wouldn't have liked it either. The Church called it "living in sin" and that was enough for them.

I think all of us kids learned that the only way to survive in our family was to lie.

Anyway, the thing is, that even after bailing my sister out of trouble over the checks, Mom told me not to say anything to my Father. She said she didn't want to upset him. As always, I did as she asked, but I never felt they gave me the same leniency they did the other kids in the family. I was always doing what I was told to do but I felt like I couldn't please my parents no matter what I did. Whether this is the truth or not is hard to say, but it certainly was the way they made me feel.

Although at the time it didn't seem like anything out of the ordinary, something happened one day when I was 18 that would change the course of my life forever.

December 9, 2006, Detroit, Michigan

I'm sitting sobbing softly in a little room someplace in the bowels of the huge MGM Grand Casino. There are no flashing lights here, no color, none of the glitz and pizzazz of the casino floor. I am shaking and want a cigarette but there is no ashtray and I'm afraid to ask for one.

If John were here he would know how to handle this. He would know what to do, but I am so scared I can't keep my thoughts straight. I'm afraid they're going to put me in handcuffs and take me off to a jail. Then what? I get to make a phone call. That's what I know from the movies. I'll call John. What am I going to tell him? What if he's out in the woods hunting and I can't get him. Will they let me make another call? Who would I call? My daughter? My mother? The attorney who handled the divorce? I don't even have his number. Maybe he doesn't take cases like this.

I don't have any sense of time. It seems like I am here forever yet for only a frozen moment. I can't make any sense of it.

Two stern-faced security guards stand near the door as if I'm a dangerous criminal who might try to escape at any moment. The third man in the room sits at the table across from me. He smiles the good-cop smile as he opens up a notebook.

"I'm going to need your statement," he says.

Statement? What statement? I don't have a statement.

"We have the video," says one of the security guards. "We have it all."

The casinos have video cameras all over the place. Everybody knows that, but does he mean he has one specifically of me playing the machines? There are thousands of them. How could they have picked me out specifically? I can hear John saying, "They've got more security there than Homeland Security."

The man at the table slides a pen from his jacket pocket and nods. "The video will give us the particulars as to your exact activities here but I have some questions for you that I'll be taking down for the record. Do you understand?"

"Yes," I say between little sobs.

"*You're married, aren't you?*"

"*Uh huh.*"

"*Where's your husband now.*"

"*Hunting. He's in the Upper Peninsula hunting. We have a place there. He goes there hunting.*"

As soon as I say that I start thinking that maybe I shouldn't be saying too much. Maybe I shouldn't be saying anything at all. Maybe I should insist on having someone with me. Maybe an attorney. I don't know anything about these things. I'm not a criminal. I've never been arrested before. Am I under arrest now? They never said that exactly but I must be.

"*It's nice up there,*" the man says. "*Good to get away from Detroit for a while. Does your husband know you're here?*"

"*Yes,*" I lied.

"*How much money did you go through before you hit the jackpot?*"

"*I'm not sure,*" I lied.

"*How much did you bring with you?*"

"*Not much. I don't know,*" I lied.

I had long since passed the point where the difference between a lie and the truth had any meaning for me.

Then: "*You're on the list. We know you are on the list. You signed it.*"

It was as though all the air had suddenly been sucked out of the room.

TWO

✦

"Why don't you come with me tonight?" Mom said. "To the Bingo. I could use the company."

"I dunno," I said. "I don't really like that kind of stuff."

"You might if you tried it."

"Sounds really boring."

"No, it's fun. It really is. C'mon I'd like you to come with me."

Every Wednesday evening over at St. Agatha's they set up Bingo games in the gym.

"It's over at the church," she says as an unnecessary reminder.

"It's still gambling."

"Yeah, but it's for a good cause. Besides the church wouldn't do anything that wasn't right if that's what you're thinking."

"I guess not."

"It's not a sin, that's for sure. All the priests can tell you that. Any money they make goes right back into the school."

"I know."

"So you'll come with me?"

"Okay,"

So I agreed only because she wanted me to, not because of the game. We got there a little early and sat at a long table which was quickly filling up, mostly with ladies Mom knew. She greeted a few of them as she showed me the cards with the numbers on them and her collection of water color daubers. She explained that most Bingo cards had 25 squares arranged in five columns so that each one has five boxes.

"The only square that doesn't have a number in it is the middle one," she said pointing out the square with the tip of a dauber. "You can see a 'B' at the top of the first column with 5 numbers always from

23

1-5 under it. The 'I' has 5 numbers between 16- and 30. The 'N' numbers are 31 through 45; the 'G,' 46- through 60; and the 'O' 61 through 75."

Some of this wasn't exactly new to me, but she was eager to show me how much she knew about the game.

"Now if you look up to the front of the hall you can see the ping pong balls, 75 of them with numbers painted on them 1-75. Most of the time they put the balls in a wire basket that somebody turns by hand and then pulls out a ball. In some of the bigger halls they play more with blowers that are plugged-in machines that blow out one ball at a time. When the balls come out they're put in a rack and that sometimes lights up that number on a big board so that everyone can see it. If you get a Bingo, you need to call it out as quick as you can and then somebody will come over to see if you've got it right. If you do, then you can go up and get your money."

We played for a few hours and neither of us won anything, but despite my reluctance, I have to admit the game was, as Mother said, fun.

I told her maybe I'd go with her another time.

One night after work I went out to the Southfield Bowl to play pinball and have a couple of beers with Madelyn, a girlfriend from Herc's. We were playing pinball for a while before I noticed a tall, dark handsome man with long dark hair tied back in a ponytail sitting at the bar staring at me.

After a while he came over to the machine with his friend and asked if they could play with us.

I have to say I was attracted to him from the first moment I saw him, but when he came up to us, it made me very nervous. I just wasn't good in situations like this. Knowing that you are timid and shy doesn't help you become less so.

I looked at Madelyn to take the lead. "Sure. Okay," she said.

"I'm Bobby," said the man who had been staring at me. "Can I buy you another beer?"

I didn't know what to say. Letting a man you didn't know buy you a drink could be unwise.

"Sure," Madelyn said before I could decide how to answer.

I guess the other man introduced himself, too, but honestly I was so nervous I didn't pay any attention.

We played pinball for a while and then went and sat at a table where we had some more beers which helped loosen me up somewhat. I wasn't really good talking with strangers. I never knew what to say and I'm sure I always came off uninteresting. Madelyn was much better at it and carried most of the conversation. We weren't talking about anything important—just working at Herc's and small things like that.

I found out that Bobby was working at a boys home for troubled teens. He was some kind of maintenance worker there. I learned, too, that he liked bowling and motorcycles but that he didn't have one.

I liked him right away maybe in part because he seemed truly interested in me and not many boys were.

Around midnight I told Madelyn that I thought it was time to go. I wasn't about to miss my curfew.

"Can I have your telephone number?" asked Bobby. "I'd like to call you sometime."

There was no way in the world I was going to give it to him. All I needed was for him to call the house. Father would have killed me.

"I'm sorry," I said. "My Father wouldn't…"

"Look," said Madelyn sensing my hesitation, "you guys want to meet us here tomorrow night? Same time?"

"Yeah," said Bobby. "That would be great. Same time, same place."

"See you then," said Madelyn.

"See you then," I repeated because I couldn't quickly think of anything else to say.

I may have been nervous but I was also excited. The next day at work I thought of him a lot and wondered if when I saw him again, would he really be as good looking as I thought, or had I invented that out of wishful thinking?

When we got to the bowling alley that night Bobby was there sitting at the bar by himself, and yes, he was every bit as handsome as I remembered. I nudged Madelyn to sit next to him. She was as spunky as I was hesitant. We ordered a couple of drinks but I made sure to pay for mine. I didn't want this to be like a date or anything. We talked for hours until they were ready to close the place. I could tell he was interested in me even though thankfully Madelyn was doing most of the talking.

"How about that phone number now? He said with a big smile.

"I can't," I said. "I really can't."

"You can find her at Herc's," Madelyn chimed in.

"Okay, yeah," he said.

He walked us to the car and then tried to give me a kiss, but I awkwardly turned it into a hug. I had never truly kissed a man before and didn't know what to do.

In the car, Madelyn teased me for being so backwards for my age. I confided in her that my problem was that I was attracted to him but I knew Father wouldn't ever allow me to see him for two very obvious reasons: He had long hair and he wasn't Catholic.

Father was very clear about who would and wouldn't get his approval. When Maura brought Jeff to the house he was okay because he was Catholic but not okay because he was Canadian. Father had rules and only his rules counted.

Bobby started dropping by the restaurant. Every time he walked in the door, all the girls looked up at this drop-dead gorgeous man. It didn't take them long to convince me to go out on a date with him. After coming up with a good phony story to tell my parents about where I was going, I finally told him I would.

We went to a drive-in movie. I was so scared I'm sure he could see it all over my face. On the way to the theatre we stopped for a six-pack of beer—thank goodness. The beer at least helped me calm my fears a little. He had me slide over to the middle of the seat so that he could put his arm around me. It felt good but strange at the same time.

I had never experienced anything like this—a man showing me positive attention. Father had never kissed me, hugged me, or told me he loved me nor, for that matter, had Mother. There were no words of praise for the children in our family.

So Bobby's attention was welcome but a little scary, too. I wasn't sure how to handle it. After the movie he drove me back to the restaurant where my car was parked. I stayed in the middle of the seat and when it was time for me to get out of the car he kissed me. It felt very awkward and I know he could tell I knew nothing about kissing. While I was driving home I felt a warm glow of satisfaction but no matter how hard I tried, I couldn't shake the ever-present sense of guilt.

After that we started seeing each other a lot. We'd go bowling, or to the movies, or sometimes to a bar. One day he asked me if I would be willing to meet his mother and sister. The idea filled me with dread but I thought it was something I should do. After work one night I stopped by his house. He was waiting for me in the driveway. When he saw how nervous I was, he took my hand and led me into the house where both his mom and sister gave me hugs. How different this was from my house. We played cards in a relaxed atmosphere which we could never have done in my house.

Later I met his three brothers. His father, though, who wasn't there, seemed to be a touchy off-limits subject. His parents were divorced and I know he didn't see his father much, if at all.

My head was spinning with all the new things that were happening to me. Someone cared about me and it felt good. I knew the time was coming when I would have to bring him over to my house to meet my parents and I was extremely worried about how that would go. I kept postponing what I knew was inevitable but eventually I got up the courage to talk to Mom about Bobby. I told her the essentials—he wasn't Catholic, he had long hair, and I liked him. I left out the part about his teaching me to French kiss. She said she needed to talk with Dad first and then she would let me know whether a visit from Bobby would be a good idea.

I guess Mom eased Dad into agreeing because a few days later she told me to come into the living room and sit down. I knew the grilling was about to start.

"Has this boy touched you?" Father asked.

"Touched me?"

"You know damn well what I mean."

"He kissed me, yes."

"That's all?"

"That's all."

"You'd better not get pregnant."

That's all he said. I was so startled by the comment I didn't know what else to say. Getting pregnant! That was the furthest thing from my mind.

Dad walked out of the room right after that.

"It's okay," Mom said. "You can bring him over. What's his name again?"

"Bobby."

Since we weren't allowed to call boys from the house, I had to wait until I got to work to call him.

When the day for the inquisition came, I left work, went home, showered and curled my hair. I would love to have put makeup on but that was not allowed either. Dad was very strict about how the girls appeared. Making ourselves look attractive was out of the question. Naturally when we were going out we all snuck around and put on makeup where Dad couldn't see us and then made sure to take it off before coming home.

As Bobby started walking up the driveway, I could see Dad checking out this boy dressed in his usual all-black clothes with black boots and a pony tail.   Dad looked at me with a what-the-hell-are-you-doing-with-this-guy look. I know a lot about being nervous, and was Bobby ever nervous. Who could blame him? Meeting Dad wasn't exactly like meeting Santa Claus. Dad shook his hand, though. That was at least a good start. A very awkward moment followed the introductions.

"I guess we'd better get going." I said after what seemed like an eternity. "It's getting dark and we're going to the drive-in."

As I was walking out the door I glanced at Dad who was glaring at me with that look of complete and utter disgust that I knew well. I figured that when I came home my parents were going to tell me that I couldn't see him anymore.

During the movies I explained a little bit about life in my house.

"It's not like Father didn't like you," I said, "it's just that he knows you're not Catholic. I had to tell him that. See, my parents expect all the children to marry someone who is Catholic, so even going out with you is, well...it gets Dad nervous."

"Hey, I can turn Catholic if that's what it takes. I don't care one way or another. I don't really have a religion anyway, so it doesn't matter to me."

For the first time I realized that he was serious about the relationship.

When I got home that night my parents were waiting up for me. They said they thought he seemed like a nice guy, but let me know in no uncertain terms that I wasn't to get too close to him because he didn't have the right religion. I didn't say anything about what he had said about converting because I didn't know where the relationship was going to go.

When he asked me to go steady I wasn't convinced it could work.

I know that most of the girls I knew were having sex but that just wasn't a priority with me. As far as I was concerned, sex was only for having babies, not for having fun. In my house "sex" was a bad word there was no talk about anything having to do with it.

"I have to tell you," I said, "that well...see, I'm a virgin and I'm not going to have sex before I'm married. I know that probably sounds stupid to you, but that's the way I am."

"That's one of the things I like about you," Bobby said. "You don't sleep around."

I know he meant that as a compliment but it made me feel really dumb.

A few months later we were in the bowling alley bar having a beer when seemingly out of the blue he blurted, "Do you want to get married?"

I knew he was going to ask me at some point but I wasn't expecting it that night so it caught me off guard. Yes, I wanted to get married because at least it would get me out of the house, but the reality is while I liked going out with him, I didn't love him.

"My parents wouldn't let me," I said. "You know that. I've got to marry someone Catholic."

"Like I said, I'll convert if that's what it takes."

We talked for a while and then I said I would marry him. This wasn't the glorious moment I had anticipated. Still, I was willing if not ecstatic.

When we met with my parents a few days later I really didn't know what they would say. We told them we wanted to get married, but not to worry because he would take the necessary classes to become a Catholic.

They grilled him a little. "You want to convert then?" asked Father looking for confirmation.

"Yeah, sure."

"You know it will take about three months."

"That's okay."

"You'll have to wait until then. You're not going to get married until you do."

"I understand that."

"Were you ever baptized?"

"No. I don't have any religion."

"What about your parents?"

"My mother doesn't go to church. I don't see my father but I don't think he does either."

"You do believe in God?"

"I guess so."

They never asked me if I loved him. All they needed was assurance that I would be marrying a Catholic. As soon as they were assured of that, they said it would be okay.

That was it. I was set to get married to a man I didn't love. I know this is supposed to be one of the great moments in a young girl's life. It wasn't.

While Bobby was taking classes three times a week to become a Catholic, I continued to work and we started planning for a June wedding.

Mom got sick and had to have an operation to remove her thyroid because of a goiter. Since Maura was living in Canada, it fell to me to take care of Debbie. I didn't mind really, as somehow it felt just like playing house.

After Mom returned home and recuperated for a while she went back to playing Bingo every Wednesday night at the church. After a couple of nights playing by herself, she asked me to go along with her. At first I didn't see how that was going to work.

"Bobby can take care of Debbie, for a while," she said.

Bobby nodded. "Sure," he said. "No problem."

He liked spending time with my Dad and this would just give him a good excuse.

If nothing else, it would get me out of the house for a few hours and away from my father.

The game was in the school gym where as usual they had set up tables for the players and a front desk with a microphone for the caller.

We bought a few cards and took our seats near some women my mother knew. She chatted with them a bit between offering suggestions to me on how to play in ways that would increase my chances of winning. Mom made it sound a lot more complicated than it really was, but I did end up winning two times that night.

Beginners luck I was told. As I was soon to learn, even the thought of winning can become addictive.

It quickly became a weekly event. Mom and I played Bingo, Bobby babysat and talked to Dad. I enjoyed the time with Mom and I know Bobby enjoyed the time with Dad. They were becoming very close.

For a couple of hours everything that was going on in my life faded away and all I thought about were the numbers needed to make me a winner. The tension that always filled the house gave way to mindless joy.

I had no idea of the direction my life was to take because of those numbers or of the strangle hold that would slowly but surely embrace me with its simple charms.

December 9, 2006, Detroit, Michigan

I am sitting at the table in the little room shaking, wishing there was a window to open. The officer and one of the male guards sit opposite. I can sense edginess flitting between them. They are not friends.

"Dump your purse out," says the security guard in a very gruff manner.

"You don't need to dump it," says the officer as if he is rebuking the guard. "Just take everything out one at a time and place what you have on the table."

The guard looks hard at him but doesn't say anything. I can tell the officer is in charge, a fact that doesn't sit well with the pushy guard.

One by one I take out everything in my purse—keys, wallet, cigarettes, bic lighter, brush, compact. Nothing here to cause concern. If they're looking for drugs or something like that, they're not going to find it. I'm a gambling addict, not a cocaine addict.

The officer, seeing my hands shaking, gives me a sympathetic look. I'm certainly not going to get that from any of the guards who appear as if they're enjoying my anguish.

I take out what little money I have left—$13.35. The guard counts it out like it was for a million dollar drug deal. The officer slides the money to one side of the table and looks into my now empty purse.

"You can put everything back," he says. "Except the money. You can leave that on the table."

Thirteen dollars! Not even worth one decent slot play.

The door opens and another guard brings in a manila envelope and hands it to the officer. "Here it is," he says.

The officer opens it and slides out a stack of money, mostly hundreds. He counts it slowly, methodically. "One hundred...two hundred...three hundred."

I realize it must be what I won on the machine.

"One thousand...one thousand one hundred...

I'd dreamt of big payouts like this, ones that take a long time to count out. Every gambler does but now that I have one, there is none of the joy I had imagined.

"Three thousand five hundred…three thousand six hundred," he says slapping the last bill down like he was playing the winning card in a poker game.

"Do you acknowledge that there is $3,600 there?"

"Yes."

"That you won $3,600 playing a slot machine in our casino."

"I don't know what I won. I guess so if that's what you say."

"That's the payout--$3,600."

"Okay."

There's something else in the envelope. He slides out an official looking sheet of paper.

"Read it carefully," he says. "It's important that you understand it completely. If you have any questions, please ask me. If not sign it on the bottom where you see your name."

It's not easy to read through tear-blurred eyes. I really can't concentrate on the details but the gist of it is that by signing I was releasing everything I had just won to the Michigan Gaming Commission.

THREE

✦

The more time Bobby spent at the house, the more my parents took to him—especially Dad. Bobby was courteous, helpful around the house, and best of all, soon he would have the right religion.

We set a mid-June wedding date. It would have to be a small wedding because we couldn't afford anything else. Since my parents could only cover a small portion of the expenses, we had to scramble for the rest. We came up with every penny we could squeeze from our jobs. His grandparents gave us the down payment for the Knights of Columbus Hall where we would have the reception, and his mom agreed to pay the bar bill.

While wedding plans were falling into place, we continued to go on dates and despite what I had told him earlier, he tried to go further than just kissing and touching. I made him stop. It felt dirty to me.

I was getting cold feet and thought about calling everything off. I was scared to death knowing I was going to have to have sex with him. I even talked to Maura about it.

"Don't be silly," she said practically laughing. "You'll come to like it."

I sincerely doubted that. Maura told me all the basics. It sounded horrible! I couldn't see myself going through with it and many nights I stayed awake worrying. There was still time to back out I kept telling myself, but I knew all the plans had already been made and lots of hard-earned money spent. I felt trapped.

Finally I got the courage to talk to Mom. I told her I was terrified about having sex. She basically told me the same thing Maura had— that in time I'd get used to it. She didn't say I'd enjoy it, just that I would get used to it.

Still, if I could have found a good way out I would have taken it, but since I couldn't, I kept myself as busy as I could with work, planning, and helping out with Debbie—anything to avoid having to think about the inevitable.

A few days before the wedding we went out for the evening and I could tell there was something on his mind.

"What's wrong?" I asked him.

"What makes you think there's something wrong?"

But I knew there was. I asked him several more times. Maybe he, too, was having second thoughts. If he was, I sure wanted to hear about them. That might solve everything.

Finally as we got home and were parked in the driveway he said. "Yeah, you're right; I do have something to tell you."

I held my breath thinking that he really was going to cancel the wedding.

"I should have told you a long time ago I know, but well…I don't know I just didn't want you to be upset with me."

"Bobby, what?"

"I'm paying child support."

"Child support! What child?"

"I don't even think he's mine."

"What are you talking about?"

"I got caught in this situation…"

"You're paying for your kid?"

"A son, but I don't really think he's mine," he repeated.

He kept saying that—that he was with this girl, yes, but the boy probably isn't his, but it was easier to agree to payments because he didn't have the money to fight it.

I started crying. This was about the last thing I had expected to hear and about the last thing I wanted to hear. I naturally assumed it had happened since we started dating.

"How could you possibly do this to me," I said between sobs.

"No, it was before I even met you. This girl, she slept around so I don't know…"

"How can you be telling me this now?"

I could see he was almost as upset as I was. "Please," he said. "I promise I'll always be true to you. This was something …I don't want you ever to think I don't love you. I do. I really do."

By now I couldn't even say anything. I just sat there crying like a spurned bride-to-be.

"This doesn't have to change anything. We can still get married."

"I don't think we have any choice," I finally managed to say as I got out of the car. "Not with three days to go."

I didn't sleep at all that night. I was upset, angry, confused. So many thoughts were rumbling around in my head—doubts about what I was doing, fear of the sex that would follow, anger over his keeping this from me, not knowing who I could turn to get away from all this.

The next morning he called and spoke with Mom for a long time. I didn't really want to talk with him, but after a while Mom handed me the phone.

"Here," she said. "You've got to deal with this."

"What are we going to do," he said still sounding very upset. "I'm really sorry. I mean that from the bottom of my heart. I should have told you I know. It's all my fault and I'm so sorry."

He must have said he was sorry a hundred times. Well, it seemed like it anyway.

"I'm sorry because I love you and I promise I will take care of you."

There was a long pause on the line before he said, "Do you still want to marry me?"

I felt incredibly cornered. If I really thought there was an honorable way out, I would have jumped at it, but the rehearsal dinner was only hours away and I didn't think I could have faced the embarrassment of calling it off at that point.

"I'll see you tonight at the rehearsal."

The rest of the day was a complete fog. I kept myself busy taking care of Debbie who by then felt like my own daughter. She was to be the flower girl and Maura my maid of honor.

At the rehearsal I couldn't even look him in the eye. The priest spoke to both families for a few moments and wished us luck. On the ride to the restaurant after the rehearsal I made sure Debbie was with us so that I wouldn't have to talk to Bobby about the night before.

After dinner, when we were finally alone he asked me to look at him and when I did I started crying

"I'm sorry," he said yet again.

"Really, is the child yours?"

"Like I told you, it's not but I couldn't afford to fight it. Mother is making the payments for me. Fifteen dollars a week."

"We can talk about it after the wedding."

This was supposed to be the happiest moment in my life and all I could feel was sadness. It was a pattern I was to repeat most of my life. It was simply easier not to say anything than to deal with reality.

On the Saturday of the wedding I woke up early. Everyone in the family except me was very excited. I was scared to death.

Because of the occasion, Father allowed me to get my hair and makeup done. When I looked in the mirror, for the first time I thought maybe I was somewhat pretty. Maybe all those years of thinking I wasn't was because I was told that or because the men in my life made me feel that way. Maybe I was too tall and skinny but my face wasn't bad. Then Mother told me I looked wonderful. Wow, I'd never heard that from her before. Of course, any thought that Dad would say something like that would have been asking too much.

When we arrived at the church I went into a room to put the wedding dress on. I was shaking because I was so scared. You should be happy I kept telling myself. But it wasn't to be. I'd just go along with the flow.

When it was time to walk down the aisle, I put my hand in Dad's arm and I thought for a moment I was going to lose my footing. I was a robot walking unsteadily. When he gave me away, he just handed me over to Bobby without a hug, kiss, or even a smile.

I went through the motions with the priest and did as I was instructed. Finally, after what seemed an eternity, the priest said, "You may now kiss the bride." I wouldn't let him kiss me deeply since that was not something you were supposed to do in public.

We walked back down the aisle, had pictures taken, and headed for the reception. Thank God there were some members of the wedding party in the car with us. When we got to hall I smiled nicely as we walked to the head table for dinner. I was hoping nobody was going to clang glasses, but of course, they did. I kept the kisses simple though.

I don't think anybody was expecting more because everyone knew how shy I was. When it came time to dance with Dad I made sure I was a little tipsy. We didn't speak during the entire dance. Bobby wasn't really a very good dancer so I didn't really feel too bad dancing with him. As the evening wore on I drank more and more, dreading what would come later. We were expected to leave early but stayed to the very end.

When there was no more delaying to be done, we went back to the tiny apartment we had rented a few weeks earlier. I was so nervous I could hardly see straight. I knew I was supposed to put on the lingerie Mom had bought me for the occasion but I didn't. I sat at the kitchen table.

"What's wrong?" my husband asked.

I told him the truth. "I'm afraid of what comes next."

"Why? It's okay. It's nothing to be afraid of."

"But I am."

Why he didn't push himself on me, I honestly don't know. All I know is I was still in the kitchen at 5 A.M. when I saw he was asleep. I lay down on the couch to get a few hours rest. My dreaded wedding night was finally over. I slept fitfully without dreaming. I didn't dare.

December 9, 2006, Detroit, Michigan

"You do know you're in deep, don't you," says the officer more as a statement of fact than as a question.

I just shake my head and begin crying hard. I am thinking of John again and how he will learn about this. I know how much I love him and I know how much I have let him down.

The officer looks at me as if he knows I'm not used to being treated this way.

"Why did you ever even come here in the first place," he asks sympathetically.

Between sobs I manage to squeeze out a weak "I don't know."

"You know what it meant when you signed out, don't you."

I collect myself a little and then after a long pause: "I was on my way to the Fairlane Mall in Dearborn when this overwhelming feeling came over me. I had to come. I don't know why. I just had to. It's hard to explain."

"And what machine were you playing?"

"Triple sevens."

"With twenties or hundreds?"

"Twenties."

"What other machines? What order did you play them before you hit the jackpot?"

I can't remember all the machines I played and in what order. I had moved around a little before I hit the jackpot. He keeps pressing me for the order of machines as if that made any difference. I tell him what I can remember which is not a lot because I'm so scared and tense. He seems annoyed at this as if I'm lying to him about something, but I'm not. Finally he moves on to other questions.

"What time did you get to the casino?"

"A couple of hours ago."

"Two hours?"

"I think it was a quarter to noon."

"You're pretty sure about that?"

"Yeah, I remember the time. It was a quarter to twelve."

"Okay, good. What type of car did you come here in?"

Why would he possibly want this information?

"A 2006 Jeep Grand Cherokee Limited Edition," I tell him. "Gray. Sort of greenish-gray.

At this point I'm not about to give him any more lies to and get into even more trouble than I'm already in.

"Where is it parked?"

"On the first level. I don't know exactly. Near the elevator. On the left side."

Now I'm afraid they're going to take my car, too.

A man opens the door. "They're ready," he says.

"Okay," says the officer. He taps his pen a few times and then tells me he's going to leave the room for a few minutes to watch the tapes they have of me playing the machines.

When he leaves, the pushy guard gives me a nasty look and shakes his head.

"Hope you had your lipstick on, sweetheart. In the videos."

I'm crying so hard I can hardly hear him.

"You're in deep shit. Hope you know that. They're going to take it all the way, you know. They'll prosecute you like you were Bonnie Parker and throw away the keys. And you know what? There's not a goddamned thing you can do about it. They always win. The casinos always win because they got big-shot lawyers and they got the judges in their back pockets. Oh yeah, they'll get you and make it stick big time."

I can see he's enjoying this. "Please, stop," I say.

"Or you'll do what exactly?"

FOUR

✦

I was completely humiliated when I awoke the morning after my wedding night. I was expecting Bobby to say something about it, maybe even show some anger, but he never mentioned it.

There was no money for a honeymoon so we went about the day as if it were just another in the life of a normal married couple. In the evening we drove to my parents' house to open the wedding presents and have dinner with them.

I got good at coming up with excuses as to why we couldn't have sex. Bobby was getting frustrated I know, but to his credit he didn't pressure me too much. We did sleep together, but there was no sex.

About two months after we were married I started thinking about having a baby and I knew what that meant, so I began slowly working myself up to it. I wanted a baby and to be able to stay home and take care of it like my mom did. Bobby's income at the boys home though wasn't enough for us to live on and I knew we'd need health insurance.

One day my aunt called Mom and told her about a job opening as a secretary in an office where my cousin worked. I didn't want to leave the restaurant because the people there had become like family to me and I knew that I was doing a good job for them. Nevertheless, I went and filled out an application and about a week later they called and said I had the job. I was to answer the phones, do a little light typing, and take calls for bank drive-through machines.

I thought I was doing pretty well when one day I walked into the office and found all the files I had arranged had been strewn across the floor.

"Your boss couldn't find the file he was looking for," said one of the other girls in the office. "He had a fit and well…you can see the result."

I was so embarrassed that I ran into the bathroom and cried. Later that day, another supervisor called me into his office. I could tell he felt bad for me.

"Just be a little more careful, honey," he said. "You're doing a good job. Just make sure you file everything in correct alphabetical order. You know how he gets. Remember, correct alphabetical order down to the last letter."

I felt better but I was always worried about losing my job. I worked real hard to memorize everything so I wouldn't make any more mistakes.

Wanting a baby I, of course, gave in to Bobby. When he was on top of me for the first time I felt him going into my vagina and because it hurt so much, I asked him not to go in all the way and he didn't. After having sex this way a few times I thought I was pregnant.

I went to see my OB but he was called out of the office to deliver a baby so I ended up seeing one of his assistants. As he was examining me, he had a very strange look on his face.

"You and your husband have had intercourse, right?" he said.

"Of course."

"It's okay, you know."

"I know."

"Because even though you are pregnant, you're technically a virgin."

I'm not sure if I saw a hint of a smile or not, but thank goodness there was no one else in the office at the time. I made sure, though, never to see that doctor again. I knew about one virgin birth; I didn't want to hear jokes about another.

Bobby and I were pretty much living loveless separate lives. All he ever seemed to want to do was to plant himself in front of the TV or go over to my parents' house. I think in reality he was using my Dad as a replacement for his. I found out from his sister that she was raped repeatedly by her father and that when his mom found out she threw him out and immediately filed for divorce. After that, Bobby, as well as his brothers and sisters, completely avoided their father.

Bobby didn't mind that I did all the cooking, cleaning, and bill-paying for both of us. He was content with me playing his mother figure and my dad substituting for his dad.

To avoid the situation I started going to Bingo more and more with my mom. As long as I took Mom out of the house and Father could spend time with Bobby, the less he seemed to take out his anger on me. This was quite a change.

By the time I was about five months pregnant, I was going to Bingo with Mom at least three nights a week. I started learning all the ins and outs of the game in all of its variety.

To play, you've got to buy at least one card, but some serious players played as many as twenty at a time. You've got to be good to do that, though, because they call the numbers pretty quick and you've got to be able to find and daub a number before more are called. It's not that easy.

They usually call the numbers about five seconds apart so you've really got to keep your attention on what you're doing. As the game moves along and cards get within one number from winning, a buzz begins to fly around the room. Real tension builds as each new number is called and you can see people inching forward in their seats and then someone yells BINGO and the tension goes out of the room like air from a balloon. It's very exciting really.

The skill in Bingo is to recognize the winning pattern before anyone else, not an easy task with 12 or more cards in play.

Since there are actually a lot of different ways to play Bingo, the caller will say what the game is before it starts. Horizontal Bingo is where you get five numbers in a straight horizontal row and Vertical Bingo is where you get five numbers in a straight vertical line. In Diagonal Bingo you have to get five numbers in a straight diagonal line that includes the free middle square. And there are lots of others.

They usually mix in different types of games to keep everything interesting. For example game one might be a standard vertical game. Game two might be a "Crazy L" where you have to hit an L pattern on any of the edges. In game three you might have to hit an X pattern. Game four might be a "picture frame" where you have to hit a square with a larger payoff if you hit all the outside numbers on a card, and a smaller one if you get it on an inner layer. Game five might be a horizontal game and game six, "railroad tracks" which means you have to get two Bingo patterns in the same direction but with a line separating them. Sometimes if the railroad is hit with fewer than 21 numbers being called you get a bigger payoff. Game seven might be a diagonal, and game eight a "double" meaning you have to get two bingos on one card. Game nine might be a "four-corner," where you need all four corner squares, and game ten "blocks of four" where you have to get four squares in all four corners, meaning a total of sixteen squares. Game eleven might be a horizontal game. The twelfth game is sometimes a grand finale "coverall" game where you have to get every square.

After a while we were playing at real Bingo halls, too, not just at the church.

How much you can win depends on how the game is set up. Say there are twelve games on the schedule with a choice of four colored cards. The green card pack might cost $4 and pay $100 to the winner; the blue pack $6 with $150 for the winner; the orange $10 for a $250 Bingo; and the red pack $12 for a $300 payoff.

Sometimes there are significant bonus payouts. For example, the coverall game might pay out five times the normal amount and often there are bonuses for quick Bingo hits where you get a Bingo in a certain number of called balls. It's possible to win thousands for a quick hit coverall, maybe even $50,000. I even heard a story of a million-dollar payout at one of the Indian Reservation games. True or not, stories like this kept us all going.

Progressive jackpots grow with each game and so the excitement in a hall builds like crazy as the jackpots get bigger and bigger.

So you can see, the games can be fun, very exciting if you get close to a big win with lots of money for the winner.

Of course, Mom and I always went to the games with an eye toward winning and sometimes we did, but there was more to it than just that. There was the pure fun of playing and the time spent with my mother. Problems from the outside world never seemed to get through the front door. A Bingo hall is like what a church is supposed to be. When you're inside all you're thinking about is what is going on there.

There's always a lot of talk among the serious players (and we were becoming just that) about whether it was better to play with a large number of cards or not. It was our kind of Bingo strategy talk. On the one hand, the more cards you played, the more money you were risking. This way, it was real easy to lose more money than you should have. Also some players who play many cards at once lose track of some numbers so that even if they win, sometimes they don't know it. Another reason not to play too many cards is that it's such hard work to follow them all that some of the fun goes out of the game.

On the other hand, many players think they can stack the odds in their favor by playing more cards. This is true, but in reality a player with one card has as much a chance to walk away with money as a player with 15 cards. What it all comes down to in the end is just plain luck. Whoever is running the game will always hold on to about 50% of the money wagered as profits. That's just the way it is and there's nothing a player can do about it.

The only thing a player can do to increase her chances is to choose cards with the smallest amount of duplication possible. For example, if you can get two cards with only two numbers the same, that's a lot better than where 4 numbers were the same. In some halls you can do this, but in some you can't choose your own numbers.

None of this mattered a whole lot to me, though. I came to love the fun of playing and the expectation of winning. And, oh yes, I did win sometimes—enough to keep me coming back anyway.

The most I ever won playing Bingo was $1,000. This was after my mother and I started going over to Canada where we met my sister to play. Their jackpots were much larger than the US and you didn't have to pay taxes on your winnings in Canada, unless you were honest at the border crossing, which nobody was. I worked up to playing a lot of cards in every game which cost around $30 per session. The Bingo session would last about two hours and then after a fifteen-minute break another Bingo session would start. A lot of the bingos in Canada would run 24/7 and if you played in American money your winnings would be paid out in American money. Mom would play about 30 cards per session. You also had the opportunity to purchase more cards for the jackpot, which would cost $1 per card. I would usually purchase an extra five cards for the jackpot. The first person to fill their card with the numbers that were randomly called would win the jackpot.

The day I won the $1000 I knew I'd be back for more.

Throughout my pregnancy, very little changed: I went to work, played a lot of Bingo with Mom while Bobby and Dad watched TV and shot the bull.

In my seventh month of pregnancy I was told I was diabetic. I had to watch what I ate and go to the hospital two or three times a weeks for a fetal monitor test. Mom always went with me and the results were always fine. The baby was moving and the heartbeat was strong.

Mom and I were becoming regulars at local Bingo halls. Any time I could get out of the apartment I would, and she obviously loved the company. Many bingoists are superstitious and tend to sit in the same spot every night so after a while when you sit at the same table each night, you get to know the people around you and chatting with a Bingo neighbor becomes part of the ritual—except of course, during the games. I was getting to know some Bingo players better than I knew my husband. I was certainly spending more time with them than I was with him. About the only thing we did together was to get the second bedroom ready for the baby.

In my eighth month we had a shower, and then as I was approaching the ninth month I was finding going to work difficult. I was having trouble with my back, because, as the doctor told me, I was so thin that my back had to hold much of the baby's weight. A couple of weeks before my due date he told me to stop working. I was concerned that the loss of money was going to be a big problem, but I was allowed to file for unemployment to see us through.

Two days before the baby was due I was at a Bingo hall with Mom and about half way through the games I started feeling cramping in my stomach.

"It's probably the beginning of labor," she said. "It'll be a while. Let's finish the game."

When the session was over, I went home but didn't go to the hospital right away because my doctor told me to time the contractions and when they were five minutes apart it would be time to go. I stayed up during the night trying to time them but they were very irregular. At about 3:00 A.M. I woke Bobby and told him I wanted to go to the hospital.

They admitted me right away and put a monitor on my belly. My contractions were still irregular but a doctor said they'd keep me anyway because of the diabetes.

In the morning after breakfast, Mom showed up and stayed for a few hours but then left because they told her it would be a while before I delivered. Bobby called his work and they told him to stay until the baby was born. I was there all day because the contractions weren't strong enough to dilate my cervix.

Around 6:00 A.M. the next morning the contractions started getting much stronger. The pain was so intense that I started crying. The nurse wasn't very sympathetic but eventually she gave me Demerol while warning me that it would slow down the delivery. At that point I didn't care because the contractions were so horrible. The next few hours were a complete blur. The hospital was a madhouse because for some reason they were delivering more babies than usual and were having a hard time keeping up. In the early afternoon my doctor came in and told me he had to leave to get some rest.

"I've been delivering babies for 48 straight hours," he said. "Don't worry, though, everything is fine with you. You're dilated but the baby hasn't descended into the birth canal yet. My replacement is very good. He'll take excellent care of you."

I was in so much pain I didn't care who delivered the baby. I just wanted it to be over with.

Later that afternoon, while a nurse was checking me, she said she'd have to go and get a doctor right away because the baby's heartbeat was slowing down. Even in my foggy state, that scared the daylights out of me. A doctor rushed in and said they were going to give me a saddle block and go in with forceps to get the baby out. They rolled me on my side and gave me a shot in the back. I immediately went numb from the waist down.

I was so scared I just closed my eyes. I didn't feel anything as they pulled the baby out and quickly put it in an incubator.

I didn't even know if it was a boy or girl until I heard one of the nurses say,

"She's blue."

I was taken to a recovery room and told not to move for six hours until the saddle block wore off. Mom came in and gave me the vital information: the baby was seven pounds and six ounces, was 22 inches long, had beautiful black hair, but had to be in a special care nursery for a while.

Mom looked very concerned about me, but I assured her I was

okay. When Bobby came in, we agreed on a name we had discussed before—Mindy—and then he went home to get some rest.

I asked to see Mindy but was told that wouldn't be possible until the next day. When they finally brought her to me I could see how beautiful she was—dark, and thin. She definitely had all of her father's features except she had my long arms and legs. It felt wonderful to hold her.

"She's a very good little girl," a nurse said. "The quietest baby in the nursery."

The nurse was right; she was a very good baby. When we got home she only cried when she was hungry or needed her diaper changed and only woke once a night for feeding. Bobby did help out with the night shift because it took a long time for me to get back on my feet.

I guess it's not all that unusual, but I was exhibiting all the signs of postpartum depression—I was feeling sad, hopeless and overwhelmed and I had little energy or motivation. I cried a lot. Bobby and I were living our usual, separate lives just as we had been before Mindy was born.

Bingo was about my only escape. The game was becoming more popular than ever and more and more churches were operating games to supplement their incomes.

I learned that Bingo goes back a long ways and was first played in Europe, but over here it caught on during the Depression because it was a good way to get away from the problems people were having. Then when the churches discovered it was a handy way to raise money it spread all over the country.

Someplace I read that by 1934 there were a reported 10,000 Bingo nights in various places across America. The largest gathering, was supposed to be 60,000 people at the Teaneck Armory in New York.

According to the story often told by serious bingoists, back in the 20s people played a game called beano with dried beans and cardboard sheets. Well, supposedly, a man named Lowe saw a game of beano being played at a carnival someplace down south and he liked it so much he brought it back to New York where he played it with his friends. It became very popular and then one day a very excited player called out "bingo," instead of "beano." Well, Mr. Lowe thought that sounded better so he began marketing games of "Bingo."

I had come to love the game as much as Mother and at the same time it gave me a chance to get closer to her than I ever had been. Also, Dad was treating me somewhat differently. I think it was because I was married and out of his hair.

All the while my marriage was getting worse. Bobby and I seldom talked except when we needed to put up a good front if family or friends were around. I went to my doctor to be put on the pill because one thing I was very sure about was that there was no way I was ever going to have another baby with him. Sex may have been something that was my duty as a wife, but I often purposely went to bed before him or stayed up late so that I could avoid that "duty."

I needed something in my life to replace the loneliness of living in a loveless marriage. Bingo supplied some of that, but I couldn't help thinking there must be something more.

December 9, 2006, Detroit, Michigan

My heart is pounding so hard it feels as if it is going to jump out of my chest. I tell myself to breathe deeply, slowly.

"You didn't really think you could get away with this, did you?" asks the guard with obvious enjoyment.

I'm not a very religious person but I can't help thinking "Please, God, don't let John call now and I'll make it up to you later."

"You can lose here, but you sure as hell can't win," says the guard. "Why don't you people ever learn that? How do you think they built this place? They built it because of idiots like you."

The guard continues with his scathing insults but I tune him out like bad music in an elevator. Breathe deeply, breathe slowly.

It seems like I'm there for hours but it is probably only about fifteen minutes before the officer returns.

"I've looked at the tapes," he says. "I got a pretty good look-see at your activities. We do that, you know. We got cameras covering about every inch of this place. Sneeze and we could say gesundheit. Anyway I've got a few more questions for you. How much money did you come with? Today, I mean. How much did you really bring with you?"

"About $600."

"Not more?"

"No. Maybe some change."

"So you must have used the ATM machine."

"Once. I used it one time to get another $250."

"Okay, good. That pretty much jibes with what we've got on the tapes--$850."

"Yeah."

"Okay, let me explain to you exactly what's going to happen from here. In a few days you'll receive a letter in the mail. It will tell you when you'll have to come downtown to have your fingerprints taken. We'll need that for evidence—to match up with when you signed out. The letter will also explain about the hearing and when you'll have to appear for that."

As bad as this is, I know the letter will make it a lot worse because there is no way I can keep it from John. Christmas is coming and I don't want to spoil the holidays. Maybe I can act normal enough that he and the girls won't know there is anything wrong. This is probably wishful thinking but at this point, it's about all I have left.

"Oh, please," I say. "Can you send the letter someplace else? Not to my house. I don't want my husband to…"

"I'm sorry. That's the way It's got to be done."

"Can't you at least hold the letter until after the holidays?"

"You don't got a choice in the matter, sweetheart," says the guard. "You'll get the letter when you get the letter. Understand?"

The officer is clearly annoyed at this. He smiles. "I'll see what I can do."

"I just can't spoil Christmas for everybody."

"I can't promise."

"I'd really appreciate it."

The officer tells the guard to call a female officer. The two of them accompany me to the elevator and then to my SUV. As I am getting in, the female officer says, "Good luck, sweetie."

I never want to hear those words again. I am still shaking so much that I have to be very careful making my way out of the parking structure. I cry all the way home. I am ashamed.

FIVE

✦

I suppose Bingo addiction is like other addictions in the sense that eventually players need to play more because they don't get the same rush from games as they did when they started playing. So Mom and I began looking for the Bingo halls that had games seven nights a week. In a city as big as Detroit, it wasn't all that hard.

The game is escapist, plain and simple. The blame for playing so much lies ultimately with me, not Mom. I didn't have to go with Mom every time she called, but the fact is she started calling almost every afternoon to ask if I would meet her and most of the time I agreed. I simply preferred to spend time with her rather than with Bobby or Dad.

It got to the point where all I was thinking about was playing the game, and when I wasn't playing I was thinking about when the next game was. When I woke up in the mornings it was usually the first thing that came to mind.

The guilt became overwhelming. I knew it was wrong, but it was a vicious cycle. Like all the other bingohaulics, I kept on playing because I always wanted to make up the money I had lost.

I never saw it coming—the addiction. It creeps up on you little by little and very slowly it puts its arms around you and squeezes so lightly you hardly feel it. It increases the pressure imperceptibly until it has you firmly in its clutches.

Yes, I was an addict and I knew it but wouldn't or couldn't admit it.

"Hi, Barbara, let's go play tonight."

"Sure, Mom."

It was easier than facing what was at home.

When my unemployment ran out we were in financial trouble which only added to my growing resentment towards my husband. He had promised me that I could be a stay-at-home mom. Clearly that was now impossible. To make matters worse he eventually lost his job because he was caught stealing supplies. He then started doing odd jobs for homeowners, but his income was so irregular that we couldn't count on it.

I was worried sick about how we were going to make it when I found out from the manager of the apartment complex where we were living that they were looking for a cleaning lady. I jumped at the chance, not because it was a great job but it was one I could do without have to go far from home. Bobby took care of Mindy when he got home and I left to clean apartments, each of which took me about four or five hours to complete.

By the time Mindy's first birthday rolled around, I was also prepping apartments for painting so I was making more. We certainly weren't flush, but we were getting by and because our schedules were different, Bobby and I weren't really seeing much of each other, and it became easier to put off the sex. He was seeing a lot more of Dad than he was of me, and as far as I was concerned that was perfectly okay.

When we got new managers I was afraid I was going to lose my job, but they not only told me they liked how I had cleaned the apartments, they also had me put in some late afternoon hours in the office answering the phone. Then one day the managers told me they were being transferred to another property and they asked me if I wanted to go with them. They were offering me free rent as well as a paycheck. I talked to Bobby and he was all for it, but the additional time the job would take meant we had to make arrangements for taking care of Mindy.

Mom agreed to babysit while I was working for $50 a week.

The new job turned out to be something I loved. For the first time I had lots of interaction with other people. For a while, everything was working well. I would drop off Mindy at 9:00 and then start work at 10:00. When Bobby got home in the late afternoon, he would pick her up.

Then about six months after the move and the new job, I was in the kitchen when the phone rang. It was Bobby.

"I'm in jail," he said rather matter-of-factly.

"Why? What happened?"

"Well, I was driving along minding my own business and some cop pulled me over. I guess because he thought I was driving too fast or something. When he ran my license he found out I had an outstanding warrant for my arrest."

"Arrest for what? What are you talking about?"

"I guess I got behind in my child support."

"You guess!"

"Yeah, well sometimes I just don't get around to it. Know what I mean?"

"No, I don't know what you mean."

"Anyway, I need to get out of here."

"Yeah, and how much is that going to take?"

"Three hundred dollars."

"You owe $300?"

"I guess so."

"How could you get that far behind without me knowing?"

"I guess they increased the amount for each week without telling me."

"What do you mean you didn't know? They couldn't increase the amount without telling you."

"Well they did."

"Did you explain that to the police?"

"They don't care. All they know is they have a warrant."

"Well, I don't have $300. Where am I supposed to come up with that amount of money?"

"Maybe your mom could loan it to you. It's got to be the whole amount though. They won't let me out with part of it."

When I hung up I called his mom, not mine.

"Well, he did know about it," she said, "because the notices were sent here and he came and picked them up."

"Can you go and bail him out?'

"Honey, I would if I could, but I just can't right now."

So I called my mom crying and told her what was going on. I think I was crying as much because I was more angry about his lying than anything else.

Mom came and picked me up and together we drove to the police station where she paid for his release. It wasn't as if she had a lot of extra cash lying around, but she always had some money squirreled away for Bingo. I didn't ask, but I think that's where she got it.

He lied and swore to me over and over that he didn't know about the increase in payments, but I knew better.

When we got home that night, I told him I wanted a separation. He thought I was just upset and the idea would pass when I settled down. I didn't press the issue then, but the more I thought about it, the more it seemed like the right thing to do. He finally realized how serious I was when one night he came into the bedroom and found me crying at the end of the bed. I told him again that I wanted a separation.

"I don't know where I'd go," he said. "I don't have any place else."

"Your mother's. You can always move back in with her."

Well, apparently she said no, because a few weeks later he moved in with his brother in a very bad part of town. It wasn't a good situation for him but I was determined that we were no longer going to live together in an unhappy marriage.

The irony of the situation is that I didn't want to live with his lies without realizing that I was on my way to becoming an even bigger liar.

My parents were anything but happy about the turn of events. They liked Bobby. They kept telling me that I had made a mistake, so as something of a compromise, I let him continue to pick up Mindy after work and take her over to my parents' house where he usually hung around for a long time. This really bothered me. They were my parents, not his, but that's not the way it seemed.

They let me know that he was like a son to them and that they would continue to invite him over for Sunday dinners.

I talked with his sister about this several times and she agreed with me.

"You should never have married him," she said to me straight out.

"I know," I said. "I suppose I always knew, but at the time I didn't exactly have a lot of boys knocking down the door to get to me."

"He's pulled the wool over your parents' eyes, hasn't he?"

"Big time."

"He's good at that."

"Yeah."

I was separated from Bobby but certainly my parents weren't. So about the only way I could have anytime with Mother without Bobby hanging around was to take her out to a Bingo hall.

By the time Mindy turned three I was becoming worried that she was getting mixed messages. Surely she could sense the tension between me and Bobby.

I can't honestly say he was a heavy drinker most of the time, but on the occasions when he did drink a lot, he could become very verbally abusive.

I finally worked up the courage to talk to Mom about everything.

"I don't like it, Mom," I said. "I don't like him hanging around here so much. I don't think it's good."

"You know he feels like a son to us, don't you?" she said stating the obvious.

"And I don't like that a whole lot."

I spoke with Bobby later than night and told him that if he still wanted to pick up Mindy every afternoon after work, he was going to have to leave my parents' house shortly after. He wasn't crazy about that but I think he knew that if he didn't agree, I was going to have to take things to another level.

Bobby, for his part, didn't even want to think about a legal separation and my parents, of course, were dead set against divorce. That wasn't something a Catholic family would ever consider.

So for a long time we went along our separate ways. I buried myself in work and Bobby did what he always did which was very little. My only salvation seemed to be the countless hours I spent hiding in Bingo halls.

When Mindy was old enough, I scraped together every penny I could find to enroll her in a Catholic kindergarten. The public school system where we lived was so awful, I felt like I had no choice. I would take her to Mom's in the morning and the bus would pick her up and return her there. Other than the cost, it was a good situation.

Mom and I were still playing Bingo regularly and sometimes we'd go bowling. He may not have been doing a whole lot else, but at least Bobby was spending countless hours babysitting.

Then when my boss asked me if I'd be willing to transfer to another apartment complex, I jumped at the chance. It meant that Mindy would be able to go to a public school near there and I wouldn't have to pay tuition. It was a great opportunity and I was looking forward to it. The only negative was that Mom was clearly annoyed that she would be losing the $50 a week I had been paying her.

On a nice weekend in June, my brothers moved me and Mindy into a new townhouse. It had three bedrooms, one and a half baths, and a full basement. It felt like a real house, a place where I could finally put down roots and I loved it.

Bobby came by to check it out and naturally, wanted to move in with us.

"No way," I said. "This comes with my job and you're not going to jeopardize that."

"I am you husband, you know," he said getting very angry.

"That may be, but we're not living together now and we're not going to live together in this place. This is mine. This is ours—mine and Mindy's. You'll have to make do on your own."

"Or what?"

"You know damn well what."

"Tell me."

"There will be…consequences."

"Then I want Mindy every other weekend."

"Every other weekend?"

"That's what I said, didn't I?"

"Okay, now leave."

"I'll leave when I'm ready."

"You're ready. Goodbye."

After he had gone, Debbie came by and helped me unpack. Finally, something positive seemed to be happening to me. The new job was good, the complex where we lived was nice and clean, Mindy was in a good school. There was a pool in front of the clubhouse where Mindy learned to swim and the complex had nice paved walks where she learned to ride a bicycle. Mindy turned out to be an excellent swimmer and I could keep an eye out for her right from my window. I met a girl there who was willing to babysit in the summers. After work I made dinner for us and then we'd go for walks around the complex or I'd watch her ride her bike.

That move turned out to be the most important thing I ever did but, at the time I didn't realize why.

December 12, 2006, Detroit, Michigan

I'm in a constant state of worry, fear, and dread. I am always tired because I can't sleep, often sweaty, sometimes nauseous. The arrival of the mailman terrorizes me. I try to keep busy with shopping and housework but I can't concentrate on anything for very long. I try to hide all of this from John. Surely, though, he can see through my facade of normalcy. It's only a matter of time.

SIX

✦

I guess to be happy you have to have something to hope for, but I'd been let down so many times in my life that I began to lower my expectations rather than risk more disappointment.

What came next for me, though, put that idea to the test.

Maybe I shouldn't use the word "luck" to describe it but that's really what it was. One day as I was working at the new complex where I had moved, I got a phone call from an older woman resident.

"There's somebody next to me playing music loud. Too loud for me. I can't do anything with that music so loud. Can you please do something about it?"

I wasn't sure how to handle the complaint but there was no one else in the office to ask so I said, "Okay, let me see what I can do."

"Because that shouldn't be allowed in a place like this," the caller went on.

"I know. You're right."

"Could you ask him to turn it down? It's boom, boom, boom like cannons."

"What unit is it coming from?"

"What?"

"The loud music, where is it coming from?"

"Sounds like everyplace."

After a few more tries I got her to be more specific. All I could think to do was to call the resident there and ask nicely for the stereo to be turned down. If that didn't work, I'd tell my supervisor and let her take care of it.

When I called the unit a man answered.

"Hi, I'm calling from the office. I'm sorry to bother you but I got a call about your stereo. One of our older residents thinks it's too loud. Do you think you could turn it down a little?"

"Oh, sure. Yeah sorry."

"Thanks very much."

"No problem."

That was it. A simple request, a simple answer and everything in my life would be different from that point on. It's funny how little unexpected things can sometimes turn out to be big things.

About a week later, the resident called again.

"Well, it's too loud again," she said. "That darn music from the same place. Don't they know other people live here, too?"

"Sorry, I gave him a call and..."

"I thought you were going to do something about it?"

"I tried, but okay, I'll go over there and talk to the man. He did say he'd turn it down."

"Well, he didn't."

"I'll talk to him."

"It's still loud."

"Okay. I'll take care of it."

At this point I wasn't sure whether the music was really loud or if this woman was exaggerating the situation. Sometimes older residents could be a little crotchety.

As I approached the building I couldn't hear anything until I got right next to the door. There was music playing and it wasn't loud but I could tell that the base was turned way up. That's probably what was creating the problem. I didn't like bothering the residents but I knocked on the door hoping that I could resolve the situation. When I had called earlier, the guy was certainly cooperative and polite.

I knocked on the door and when it opened, I almost fell over backwards. I was standing in front of an absolutely gorgeous man roughly my age. He was tall, well-built, and had beautiful long curly blondish-brown hair. I've seen enough movies where the girl meets someone like this to know that it can take her breath away. Well, that's exactly what happened to me. I'm sure at that moment I looked like a fawning young school girl. When I regained my composure I introduced myself as the manager.

"You know that resident I called you about a week or so ago? Well, she complained again."

"Oh, sorry," he said.

"I don't think it's really too loud though. I think it's probably just the bass. Maybe you could ..."

"Absolutely. I'll just have to live with a little more treble."

"If that's okay."

"No problem. Come in. I'll do it right now."

I took two steps into the apartment and then quickly backed out. I was truly shaken up.

"Come on in a minute. It's okay. I could get you a cup of coffee or something."

"I can't really."

"Sure you can."

"I shouldn't, though."

"I'm not going to bite."

"I'm the manager so I can't really make friends with the residents."

He had a big smile on his face. "I understand."

"So if you'll just lower the bass a little..."

"Consider it done."

"Thanks."

"No problem."

"I've got to get back to the office. In case somebody calls."

"Okay, bye."

As I was walking back to the office I had the distinct feeling he was watching me, making me both uncomfortable and excited at the same time.

Had it not been for the heavy stereo bass I might never have met John and who knows where my life would have gone. I guess life can be so...accidental.

Throughout the summer John frequently stopped by the office and asked me to go out with him.

"I really can't," I told him the first time.

"Really you can't?"

"I'm not allowed to get personal with the residents."

"Says who?"

"It's part of my job description."

"Well, maybe during work hours, but believe me, you can do anything you want on your own time. No one can stop you from doing that. Ask your supervisor. You'll find out."

"Besides, you're married," I said.

"Where did you get that idea?"

"It's on you lease contract. I looked it up?"

"So you are interested?"

"No I just...I have to file leases so I...I see details sometime."

John flashed that big smile of his. He knew I was fishing for an answer. "Well, just so you have the details straight," he said, "for your information only, I'm not married."

"It says so on your..."

"Yeah, I know, but just between us, that's not true."

"Really?"

"It's what we told the old manager—me and my... girlfriend. Look, I knew I would never be approved for a place on my own, so we said we were married. Nobody ever checks those things, so it was just something we said so that I could get approved."

"Well, I am?"

"You are what?"

"Married."

"I never see you with a guy."

"We don't live together."

"So you're on your own?"

"Look, I really can't get involved with anyone right now, especially someone with a girlfriend."

John was nothing if not persistent. He continued to ask me out and I continued to tell him no. It certainly wasn't because I didn't want to go out with him, it's just that there were too many complications.

"I kicked her out," he said one day.

"Your girlfriend?"

"I caught her sleeping with an old boyfriend."

"Uh oh."

"So now will you go out with me?"

I still turned him down because I honestly thought that I'd get in trouble if it was known that I was seeing a resident. This place was just so perfect for Mindy and me that I didn't want to mess it up. Oh,

I thought about John a lot and I really wanted to be able to say yes, but I was afraid to for two very different reasons: I didn't want to lose my job, and honestly I thought he was way out of my league. He was confident, smart, and witty—all the things I wasn't.

Then about every other day when I got home after work there would be flowers and cards at my back door. This was easily the most romantic thing that any man had ever done for me.

By August that summer I was very busy getting Mindy ready for first grade. She was so excited about going to a school with her friends from the complex.

I was getting to know some of the other parents of kids Mindy played with. One was a single mom with two daughters. She told me all the ugly details of the messy divorce from her husband who left her one day for another woman. She was constantly struggling to make ends meet.

"You need to divorce that jerk you're married to," she said to me one day while we were sitting at the pool watching our daughters. "It boggles the mind that you don't."

"My parents wouldn't like it. We're Catholic."

"Look it's your life not your parents'."

"I know."

"So you're miserable because you don't want to upset your parents?"

"It's just the way I am, I guess. I don't want to make waves."

She looked at me as if I was out of my mind. "What about that guy you're seeing. John isn't it?"

"I'm not seeing him!"

"All those flowers…"

"Now you're embarrassing me," I said.

"He's really good-looking."

"He is, isn't he?"

"You got that right."

"I can't go out with a resident."

"Says who?"

"Because of my job."

"Don't be ridiculous. Of course you can. Ask your supervisor. I bet she'll tell you it's okay."

I was very tempted but very wary, too. One day I got up the courage to ask my supervisor about it. I made sure to let her know that I was just asking and that I hadn't dated him at all.

She laughed at the question. "Sure, you can date any resident you want. Whatever gave you the idea you couldn't? Just so long as you don't give any resident special treatment you're free to see anyone your little ol' heart desires."

"Really?"

"Really."

The opportunity came in mid-September. I was walking in the complex when he drove up in his pickup truck.

"Well, have you spoken to your supervisor yet?"

I know I shouldn't have been, but I was so nervous. "Yeah, I asked her."

"And...?"

"She said it was okay just so long as I don't give you special treatment?"

"Actually I am looking for special treatment."

"You are?"

"Absolutely. You don't date all the residents, do you?"

"I don't date any of the residents."

"I think it's time you start. How about it?"

When I agreed, he winked and said he had to get going but that he'd give me a call to make arrangements.

On Friday he did call.

"You like Phil Collins and Genesis?"

"Sure."

"I've managed to get my hands on a couple of last-minute tickets for their concert tonight."

"Well, actually I was going to go out with one of my girlfriends."

"So that means you've already got a baby-sitter lined up?"

"My husband has my daughter this weekend."

"Perfect. But we've got to get going. The concert starts in 45 minutes. Okay? I'll come by in 15 minutes."

Since I had planned to go out, I had already showered and curled my hair. All I needed to do was tell my girlfriend and put on some makeup. "Yeah, okay," I said hoping I was covering my nervousness.

On the dot fifteen minutes later he was at my door. I didn't let him in but told him I was ready.

Being the perfect gentleman, he opened his truck door for me—something Bobby never did. He had a cooler in the back seat and asked me if I would like a drink. I took a beer to calm my nerves.

I felt like I was in a dream from which I would awake at any moment. I was so filled with doubt. Why would this handsome man be interested in me? I was a plain, gawky woman, and as was becoming very obvious, I wasn't good at small talk. I think he quickly figured that out because he carried most of the conversation.

When we got to the concert, he took my hand and told me the tickets were on the main floor. I don't know what they cost, but it must have been a lot. I had never been to a concert like this, let alone on the main floor.

We bought a couple of beers and when a woman walked by with roses, he bought one for me. He was the perfect gentleman and I felt so good, so secure with him. The concert was wonderful and since I knew most of the songs I even started singing along a little. When it was time for more beer, I said I would go and buy them. He objected, but I insisted partly because it was a good excuse to go to the bathroom and partly because I thought I should contribute something to the evening.

After I bought the beer, I got turned around. I had no idea where our seats were. I was up in the bleacher section and couldn't even see a way to get down to the main floor. Instantly I was in a state of panic. What if I couldn't find him at all? He had the ticket stubs so I couldn't even look to see the seat numbers. I felt like a complete idiot. Then to make matters worse, as I turned around, I slipped and fell. The beer went flying and I hit my shin so hard I thought I had broken my leg. What had started out as a dream evening now looked like it had turned into the nightmare I had feared.

A man helped me up. "Are you okay?" he said.

"I'm fine," I lied and limped back towards the beer counter. I don't know which was worse, the pain in my shin or the pain of embarrassment. All around people were looking at me, something that always made me uncomfortable. I reached down and felt my shin. It wasn't broken but it ached. I hoped I could walk normally enough that John couldn't notice. Assuming I could even find him, I certainly wasn't going to tell him he was dating a klutz who wasn't smart enough to find her seat at a concert.

When I bought two more beers, the panic in my eyes must have been obvious because an usher came up to me and asked if I needed help. I did my best to describe where I thought I was sitting, and eventually we managed to find it. By this time the concert was at its frenetic peak and everyone was standing on chairs.

"You okay?" John shouted above the music. "You were gone so long…"

"I'm fine," I said as he helped me onto my chair which wasn't as easy as it should have been because of my leg.

"Great concert!" he said.

"It sure is," I shouted.

As the concert ended he made sure we didn't get separated in the exit crowds by holding me by my waist. Did he sense that I had gotten lost or was that just him being the gentleman he was? I hoped it was the latter.

When we got to my place he kissed me like I had never been kissed before and I loved it.

Then he asked me if I would like to meet him for breakfast in the morning. I told him I would. Yes, he was every bit the gentleman.

"I'll call you in the morning, then. What time would be good?"

"Maybe about eight."

"Eight it is. Good night."

The next morning I woke early—probably from anxiety. I got ready and sipped coffee while the clock slowly ticked towards eight. Would he really call? I thought he might but I wasn't sure.

At eight on the dot the phone rang. "Ready?" he said.

"Yep."

A few minutes later he arrived and we headed to his favorite little restaurant. While we were waiting for our order, I told him about my marriage and my daughter; he told me about how he kicked out his ex-girlfriend.

"She's already cleaned out her stuff. She's gone. Believe me, it's over. It's been over for a while really."

I was eager to find out more about this polite, good-looking man, who was paying attention to me even if I didn't understand why and he seemed eager to tell me.

He had grown up in the Dearborn Heights area, a suburb of Detroit, as the fifth of six children in a closely-knit Polish family. His father was a good athlete from Pennsylvania who thought he was going to play professional football but when he was tested it was determined he had type 1 diabetes. So he traded his helmet for a wrench and went to work for Ford where he eventually moved up into a supervisory role.

Like me, all of the kids in John's family went to Catholic school for the early years but then transferred to a public school after the eighth grade.

"I was a bit of a trouble-maker in school, I have to admit," John confessed.

"That's hard to imagine."

"Mom kept getting calls from the school, and it was always the same complaint—'John isn't paying attention in class.'"

"Were you?"

"I always thought I knew the stuff. Mostly I was bored. I'll tell you what did interest me, though. I loved taking things apart and putting them back together again. Leave something lying around in the garage and I'd probably dismantle it—a fan, a radio, a mixer—it didn't matter what. I was curious about how things worked. Most of the time I got them back together again, too."

"Most of the time."

"Almost always. I was pretty careful, pretty methodical."

All four of his sisters went on to work at the Ford plant but John didn't want anything to do with that. When his parents bought the house behind them, John helped turn it into a duplex and the attached two-car garage was where John and his friends worked on cars for hours on end, often figuring out ways to make the family car go faster.

"Mom thought working on the duplex would keep me busy and out of trouble."

"And did it?"

"Busy, yes. Out of trouble, well, mostly. We rented the duplex out to lots of different people over the years. Even some Red Wings players."

His memory of childhood was a positive one. The family was

always doing things together, a lot of it involving outdoor activities like hunting and fishing and going out in the family boat.

"Dad let me drive it when I was nine. Boy was I excited about that."

When John was 17 his father died and so John took on the role of father to his younger brother. I could certainly identify with that part of his story, but not with the happy childhood part. It was nice to hear about growing up happy but at the same time it made me feel a little melancholy about mine and maybe a little jealous.

John began chuckling at his own recollections. "We were always building things—me and my brother. We built sheds, forts, all sorts of contraptions. Even a house once."

"You built a house?"

"A tree house for kids. And a big shed next to the house. That burned down one day. Someone—who shall go nameless—had left a candle burning while we were all at a wedding."

"Naughty boy."

"Oh, then there was the time I tried to install a phone in my bedroom and accidentally connected it to the alarm system which, of course, brought the police running. Mom had to explain that it was only the 'boy genius' screwing up again."

"Did you do that a lot—screw up?"

"Not really. Well there was a time when I was very young that Dad gave me a hammer and a little piece of wood to keep me busy while he was doing something or other. Well that got boring after a while so I took some nails and hammered them into our new garden hose. I guess I thought we needed a soaker."

"Did you catch hell? I sure would have."

"No, Dad did for not paying closer attention to me. Mom let loose on him something awful."

It was fun to hear about a happy childhood and I wish I could have shared cute stories of growing up, but really I didn't have many, so mostly I listened. What could I have offered? Stories of being beaten by Father or molested by my brother?

He told me about working in a muffler shop for a number of years, starting when he was just fifteen. The owner liked his work so much that he even let John run the shop in the evenings. Then he went to work for a car and truck dealership where after a short time they put him on the semi-trucks, which was the best paying job you could get as a mechanic. When he moved into the complex with his girlfriend he took on some additional work with an electrician who taught him a lot about the trade. This gave him the idea of working for himself. He was so good at working on machines and things that he thought he could start his own business handling all types of repairs. His first job was for the Garden City Schools, working on their electrical and plumbing.

"Well, that's what I'm doing now," he said, "and you know, I'm pretty good at it."

"I bet you are."

"You break it, I'll fix it."

"Does that include broken marriages?"

"Depends on whose."

That evening we went to a bar where we spent a wonderful evening drinking and dancing.

"Boy, it sure doesn't take much to get you tipsy," he said.

"I should have warned you, I'm a cheap date."

After we closed the bar he asked me if I wanted to go back to his apartment. I don't know which of us was more surprised when I said I would.

When we got to his place he took my hand and I followed him into his bedroom. He had a king-sized waterbed with mirrors above it. I was so nervous I was afraid I'd start shaking and the thought of watching myself in the mirrors made it even worse. But then he started kissing me and I forgot about the mirrors. He was bringing out feelings I never knew I had.

"You're so beautiful" he said as he kissed me on the breasts.

I felt so aroused but also so guilty.

"Are you on the pill?"

"Yes."

He could tell how nervous I was and said he thought it was cute that I was so naïve. That relaxed me a little and he certainly was being as gentle as he could.

He started kissing my belly and slowly moving down to my private area. My initial reaction was to close my legs real tight.

"Have you ever had an orgasm?" he asked.

"No."

"Making love takes two people."

He kissed my private parts and then his penis went inside me and I did have an orgasm, and yes, it was wonderful.

When it was over I told him I had never felt like that before and I could see that he was very happy. We fell asleep in each other's arms.

In the morning I was back to my shy self.

"You have a lot to learn," he said.

He made me breakfast and gave me one of his shirts to put on. I went home a different person. Now I knew what it meant to be in love.

All the next day I couldn't help feeling that he might not call again. It was a stupid reaction really, but I couldn't help it. Was this what they call a one-night-stand? Did I submit too easily? Maybe I was just another one of his conquests in a long string of conquests. I was angry at myself. A little while ago it had all seemed too good and now it all seemed potentially so wrong. What is the matter with me? Why did I ever think a man like that could really be interested in a skinny, painfully shy, ho-hum girl like me?

The doubts were still circling around me like vultures ready to swoop in for the kill when the phone rang.

"How about dinner tonight?"

"Yeah."

"I know a great place for dinner."

After I had been seeing John for a while, I decided it was time he met my daughter.

"But it's got to be a secret—my seeing you," I told him. "Other than Mindy. I want her to know, but not anybody else."

"Why? We're not doing anything wrong. You're separated. You're not seeing him."

"I don't trust him. I'm afraid he'd hold it against me…"

"And do what?"

"Try to take Mindy away."

"He can't do that."

"Maybe, but I don't want to even give him the chance."

"Okay, then. I don't think you have anything to worry about, but it'll be our secret."

"Thanks."

I was really eager to get John and Mindy together. I wanted Mindy to be proud that her mother was seeing someone like him. Maybe I hadn't always done a lot to make her feel that way, but I knew she would like John. How could she possibly not?

Of course, she did right away. We went to a place he knew that had a penny candy store and little ducks that followed her around. He was a very outdoors person and she seemed to respond to that. It wasn't long before she was coming home from school every day and asking if we could go over to John's apartment where he usually had ice cream and rented movies ready for her.

On Halloween we had a party in the clubhouse. Everyone was in costume. My girlfriend even talked me into wearing a bumble-bee outfit that I was sure revealed too much but she assured me it was okay. John said he'd be there, too, but as the party wore on there was no sign of him. This wasn't like him so I was worried. Had something happened to him at work or was this his way of saying it was over?

I'm something of a worrier anyway but now I was getting a little frightened. I started thinking back over the last few days. Had I said something to upset him? Were there little hints that I missed suggesting that he was losing interest? I really couldn't think of anything.

As I was standing at the bar, someone who had been there for a while dressed as the Grim Reaper started starring at me. It took me a moment before I realized it was John.

"Oh, my God," I said taking a step backward. I was so embarrassed, but then that isn't exactly an emotion that was foreign to me.

He kissed me. "You look beautiful," he said. "The most beautiful bumble bee I've ever seen."

Everybody laughed. The secret was certainly out but at that point I didn't care. I was going with somebody who loved me and that cancelled out everything else. If Bobby was going to make an issue of it, then we'd just have to deal with whatever came.

After the party we went back to my apartment and for the first time, he was in my bedroom.

"What is that?" he said, pointing to my bed.

"What does it look like?"

"I'm not sure. There are two by fours…"

"Instead of a box spring."

"Somebody could get hurt in here."

Well we tested my improvised box springs and neither of us got hurt—in fact, quite the opposite.

I was quite head-over-heels infatuated with John but I continued to worry that I would lose him because he'd come to realize that I wasn't worthy of him. Then, too, there was the issue of my married status. I didn't want to upset my parents by considering a divorce but I sure as heck didn't want to lose John. So I decided that I would test the waters of divorce as the lesser of the two concerns. One of our residents was a lawyer so I told him my story and asked what he thought. When he said I should go ahead with divorce proceedings I told him I didn't have a lot of money, but he said he'd work for a small fee.

"Check with your husband," he said. "See if you can work out the financial arrangements on your own. It's a lot easier and a lot cheaper that way."

I knew there was no way in the world that I would ever be getting back together with Bobby but I was scared to death to talk with him about this. I knew it would lead to a confrontation, something I was never good at handling. I was so frustrated because I wanted to move forward in my relationship with John but at the same time I hated the thought of the inevitable argument that surely would follow.

After making up excuses to myself to delay the inevitable, one day I decided I would just have to summon the courage to do it. I was nervous all day waiting for him to come over. Of course, he was late.

"Look," I said to him, when he eventually arrived. "It's been six years since we lived together so I was thinking it is time for us to get a divorce."

I was right about his reaction. He was furious.

"Goddammit, we're not going to get into that. Not now, not ever."

"Why? We're never going to get back together. We both know that."

"I don't know that!"

He was shouting and throwing his arms around so wildly I thought he was going to knock over the table lamp.

"Well, I do."

"You don't know what's going to happen down the road."

"I know that's not going to happen."

"Besides I can't afford more child payment. I can hardly afford the damn payments I've got now."

We went on like this for some time before I finally got him to calm down a little.

"Look, I talked to a lawyer and he said we wouldn't ask for child support for the past six years and only the minimum from now on."

"I don't have the minimum. You damn well know that. And I certainly can't afford a lawyer. Not even a cheap one. Damn it all, Barbara!"

"You won't have to pay any lawyer fees if you don't contest the fact that I want full custody of Mindy."

"Full custody!"

"Absolutely. This is the best place for her. I think you know that."

I hated this kind of encounter, but I was proud of myself for finally standing up to him.

"That's bullshit."

"She's happy here. We have a nice place and I have a good job. What do you have to offer her?"

"I'm her father."

The argument went on for some time, but eventually he realized I was right and he agreed.

A few months later I went to court. I told Bobby not to show up because if he did he would have to pay for his own attorney. He said he'd stay away just so long as I made sure he wouldn't be back-charged for the last six years.

John went with me but stayed outside in the hall while I went in with the attorney to see the judge. When I got in there I thought I was going to faint. The courtroom had no windows so it was very stuffy and I started shaking.

Although I wanted the divorce, I dreaded this day. The very idea of having to face a judge made me very anxious. In imagining the experience I assumed the judge would be a white-haired, stern-looking man who would see me as a failure because I couldn't make my marriage work. Was I ever wrong about that! The judge was an attractive blonde woman, who, I think, immediately saw how nervous I was.

She asked me all sorts of questions which made me even more so.

"Are you pregnant?"

"No," I answered.

"Why isn't your husband here? It's normal for the husband to be here."

"He doesn't have the money for an attorney."

"This is important. He should look after his interests."

"I've talked to him about all of this and we're in agreement."

"I see you're not asking for child support for the last six years."

"No."

"Why not?"

"It's what we agreed."

She asked lots of other questions which I answered as best I could, and then all of a sudden she said, "Okay, I'll grant the divorce."

I couldn't believe that's all it took. I had worried for six years about nothing. Now I felt like the world had been lifted off my shoulders. I still had the issue with my parents, but as John had always said, it was my life and I needed to live it as I saw fit, not as they did.

When I got out to the hall where he was waiting, he hugged me and I started crying out of happiness.

"What's wrong, honey?" he said. "Didn't it go well?"

I wiped the tears away. "It went great. For a change, these are tears of happiness."

As we walked out of the courthouse he said, "To celebrate, I'm going to buy you a present."

"Really? What."

"A new bed. A single woman shouldn't have to have hers held up by two-by- fours."

Within a couple of months we started living together, but not until after he agreed he would have to finish his lease even if he wasn't living in his apartment. I remembered what my supervisor had told me about showing preferences to any tenant. Mine was a three-bedroom, 2-bath townhouse that I got rent-free because of my job, and since his was only a one-bedroom unit, of course, he moved in with me and he paid rent on his empty one for a year.

Mindy jumped for joy when I told her that John was moving in. By this time I had been promoted to property manager and hired my best friend Denise to work in the office. I had known her since the days when she was dating Bobby's brother. We lost contact when she stopped seeing him but some years later I ran into her in the laundry room after she had gotten married and moved into the apartment complex where I was living when I first married Bobby. We remained the best of friends. How vital this friendship was I would come to learn in a few years, when she would come to my aid during the toughest time in my life.

I was determined to be a good property manager and worked hard at it, but one problem that kept coming up was that the HVAC units that supplied the heating and cooling for each apartment were located in small closets and were frequently breaking down. Apparently the model we had wasn't very common and the company we paid to repair them wasn't very good. As a result, I frequently got calls from residents about the units. So when John said he could repair them, I let him work on a few and from that time on, I never got complaints. He could figure out anything and tell me if someone was overcharging me for something or that a certain repair would fix the problem. I introduced him to the owner and the owner tested him on several different projects. When he started saving the company money with repair versus replacement projects the owner welcomed him as a regular contractor.

I was able to pull a few strings with the main office and John began doing miscellaneous jobs at several different apartment complexes. Before long, people were calling him to handle jobs that no one else seemed to be able to complete. He was really very talented when it came to looking logically at a technical problem and then very calmly coming up with reasonable solutions. He was on his way to developing a very profitable business.

In early spring we went away for a long weekend. First we stayed in a beautiful old hotel and then went on to a cabin that he and his father had built deep in the Upper Peninsula woods. It was like going back in time—no water, no electricity. That night, after riding his four-wheeler and eating a wonderful dinner he cooked, we went to bed on a fold-out couch. We made mad love and fell asleep together. When we woke up the next morning we saw that we had fallen asleep with our private body parts together. Everything had dried up during the night. I felt ashamed, but when he flashed his big smile it all turned to happiness. On the way home we stopped at several places he wanted me to see—lovely rivers, dramatic gorges, scenic overlooks.

It was a magical trip, but as we got close to home, reality began setting in. How could a man like this show me such affection like I had never known before? Once again, no matter how hard I tried, I couldn't shake the nagging feeling that I wasn't worthy of it. Surely my happy new world would come crashing down at some point. Maybe I wasn't meant to be a happy person.

My parents were still upset over the divorce so I hadn't dared tell them John and I were living together. We started going over to their house for Sunday dinners, and they were warming up to him but we were careful to skirt around the living situation.

More and more, Mom was pressing me to accompany her several times a week to regular Bingo games and I can't say I resisted much.

One weekend John asked me what I wanted out of life.

"What do you mean?" I responded.

"What would make you really happy?"

"I am happy."

"For the long term."

"Honestly, I don't have a lot of expectations really."

That was absolutely true. I had learned that if you don't expect too much out of life you won't be disappointed and I had already experienced enough disappointments for one lifetime.

"Well then, what are your little expectations?"

"I'd like a house and I'd like to be a stay-at-home-mom."

"Is that all?"

"It's all I can think of?"

"You're easy to please."

"Am I?"

"And I can do that."

From his pocket he took out a beautiful diamond ring. "Will you marry me?" He slipped the ring on my finger and we hugged and kissed.

"Yes, yes, yes."

We had talked about this a few times and John said his wild

bachelor days were over and he was ready to settle down, so I wasn't surprised that he asked, just surprised that it was that soon.

Life can be hard to figure out sometimes. How I could attract a man like this I will never know, but I was overwhelmed by his offer and even if I wasn't sure I could live up to who he may have thought I was, I was determined to try.

One sticky problem worried me. We were both raised Catholic but since I had been married, and he hadn't, I didn't think we could be married in the Church and this meant my parents would be even more upset than they already were. So I made an appointment to see the pastor of the church. He was a short, round man who peered over his glasses as he asked me lots of questions:

"Have you been seeing someone else?"

I wasn't sure what answer he would like to have heard, but I wasn't about to lie to a priest. "Yes," I said. "A man named John, but he's a Catholic, too."

"What about your ex? Is he seeing someone, too?"

"I don't know. Probably."

"When you were together, was he verbally or physically abusive to you?"

"When he drank too much he'd get abusive sometimes, call me names and things like that."

"But he didn't hit you."

"No."

These sorts of questions went on for some time and made me feel uncomfortable.

"Anything else you want to tell me?" he said finally as he took his glasses off and pinched the bridge of his nose.

"We didn't consummate our marriage on our wedding night. Does that make any difference?"

"Well, I think from everything you've told me you've got a good chance to be granted an annulment from the Church."

"Really?"

"I'm going to give you some paperwork to fill out. Take it with you and get it back to me when you can. I'll also need letters from two people who know you well who can verify everything you've told me here today."

"Like who?"

"That's up to you."

"I could ask my little sister and my mother. Would that be okay?"

"That will be just fine."

I went home, filled out the paperwork, and arranged for the letters. After a while I got a letter from the Catholic Archdiocese saying that my marriage was annulled. It was so simple I don't know why I had been so concerned about it.

John, who hadn't even known I had started the process, was delighted. When I called Mom to tell her we could get married in the Church I was crying with happiness because I knew it would please her.

Still, doubt hovered. Everything in my life seemed to be going well—maybe too well. Happiness always seemed to be a part-time visitor with me.

John thought that it would be wonderful if we could all take a trip to Disney World in Florida. The idea is that we would go with his sister, brother-in-law, and their two children. Mindy was out-of-her-mind happy.

When I told my parents of our plans, they were irate. Father started calling me names again just as he had when I was younger. The very thought that John and I were going away with Mindy as a family when we weren't married infuriated them both. Their values were the ones they had learned from the Church and they weren't negotiable. The fact that John and I loved each other counted for less than Church rules.

"You just try to take your daughter out of the state and your mother and I will file for custody."

"What are you talking about?"

"We'll get custody of Mindy in a heartbeat."

"Why? We're not moving, we're just going on a vacation."

"Are you just stupid or what?"

"Dad, it's just…"

"You've always been stupid. Why should you change now?"

I hung up the phone which I'm sure just made him even more angry but I was getting to the point that it affected me less than it used to and John's support was a big reason. Still, it bothered me enough that I started sobbing.

"Don't worry about it honey," John said. "They can't take her away because we're going on vacation."

"Dad said they could."

"He says a lot of things that aren't true."

"But he's got me worried."

"Call your lawyer—the one who did the divorce. He'll tell you. There isn't a way in the world that you're going to lose Mindy because of a Mickey Mouse trip."

Despite John's assurances, I wasn't completely convinced. At least I wasn't going to take the chance if there was any possibility of an ugly custody fight.

"Look honey," the lawyer told me on the phone, "your parents don't enter into this at all. They have no rights in the issue. The only person who could even possibly try for custody would be your ex-husband and since his living conditions are anything but stable, there isn't any judge in his right mind who would grant him custody."

"But if there's a chance. Even a little one…"

"I'd suggest you call Bobby and tell him you're taking Mindy out of state for a few days. Tell him you're going to Disney World. That way he can't claim you took her in secret or that you were trying to hide her from him."

The situation made me nervous and I couldn't escape the feeling that something bad was about to happen.

I called Bobby just as the lawyer said and told him.

"I don't give a shit where you go," he said, "just as long as I don't have to pay for it."

"My parents said they'd file for custody if I went."

"Ain't gonna happen."

"That's what they said."

"They can't get custody before I do. No way, and I told you, I don't care. You got the money to waste on Disney World, be my guest."

The trip to the Magic Kingdom was everything I could have wished for and more. We rented a brand new motor home and took turns driving so that we wouldn't have to stop. It was the first time I'd ever been out of Michigan and the first time I'd ever been on a real family vacation.

Of course, the kids were so excited they didn't sleep much on the way down. When we got there, they went on just about every ride in the place. Mindy noticed Tigger, but like me, she was rather shy and was afraid to go up to him. Finally, I convinced her to stand next to the affable tiger for a picture which remains to this day, one of my proudest possessions. As we left the park, my eyes teared up with joy. We were all exhausted but deliriously happy.

At our campsite we roasted marshmallows around a fire and talked about the day. Although I never experienced it, this is how I imagined childhood should be.

On the drive home, we hit an ice storm in dense fog and the motor home nearly slid off the highway. The kids never even woke up. They were probably happily dreaming of the magic they had just experienced. I was just so happy I could give Mindy something I never had.

By the time we got home my happiness turned to angst. I knew what lay ahead—dealing with my parents. I waited a few days before calling Mom. When I did, my sister answered and said Mom wouldn't talk to me. The next day I called again and she still wouldn't talk to me. This went on for six months.

John couldn't understand my relationship with my family and I couldn't really explain it to him because I didn't completely understand it myself. I did think, though, that what really upset her was that I was spending more time with John than with her. She was jealous of John and took it out on me. I don't think she wanted me to be happy if it meant limiting my time with her.

No doubt she was trying to control me by withholding her approval, but through John's help I was certainly becoming more independent and learning about a whole new world I never knew existed.

"It's hard for me to see it, I guess," John said, "because I don't have anything in my background to compare it to."

"I know."

"My family gave me unconditional love but yours seems always to be conditional."

"I can't help it. That's just the way it is."

"Maybe you need to move on. You've got Mindy and she's a great kid, and you've got me. Let your parents go. All they seem to do is make you crazy all the time anyway."

"You know, I wish I could, but my mother...I can't stand her not talking to me. I don't know why, but I need her somehow."

"She sure as hell doesn't act like she needs you."

"That's exactly what she needs...or thinks she needs."

"You stress too much over her."

"My dad's got her all..."

"There's only one way she's going to get back together with you."

"I know."

That night I called and finally managed to get her on the phone.

"There's a new Bingo hall I heard about that's got games seven nights a week," I said. "I thought maybe you'd like to go with me."

There was a short silence on the line, and then: "Okay."

"I'll pick you up."

"Okay."

Bingo and a mother's love together again. She never mentioned the Disney World trip during the entire Bingo session. The message was clear: She would forget the incident but only on her terms. If I acted in a way that she approved and expected, she would behave towards me as she had when I was younger. It was becoming increasingly more difficult to balance my new life and still keep my mom satisfied.

So, just as long as I continued to spend time with her playing Bingo, she would show me her equivalent of love.

As our wedding date neared, John began building a house on a piece of property that he had taken care of for his mother. I was thrilled. Just the idea of having my own house was like a dream come true.

It was the house he envisioned when he was a kid. He had dreamed about it, sketched it, planned it from the foundation up and that's the way he was building it. Every night and all weekends were dedicated to building. The house was to be about 3,000 square feet with 3 bedrooms and 2 1/2 baths. There would be a big hot tub in the master bath. It would also have an office area, a fully equipped kitchen with breakfast nook, a living room with a fireplace, and a dining room. Next to it would be a 2½-car attached garage with enough room for a shop that

John could tinker in. Compared to the little house in which I grew up, it was a castle and John my knight in shining armor.

My parents said they couldn't (or wouldn't) pay anything towards the wedding but I didn't care. This time it was so different: I was never in love with Bobby like I was with John. I couldn't wait for the day regardless of how much money was spent on the reception. I'd have been happy without one.

The house wasn't ready by the wedding day but my boss said I could stay at the townhouse until it was.

As the wedding began I was shaking. This time it wasn't because I was frightened or nervous, it was because I was so excited. Still, the nagging question in the back of my mind: why would this wonderful man want to marry me? I wanted the ceremony to be over quick in case he changed his mind. As I started down the aisle I took my father's arm and then when we had almost reached the front of the church, for the first time in my life that I could remember, he gave me a little kiss. For a moment I was taken aback. He had never shown any positive emotions towards me before. The rest of the ceremony was something of a blur seen vaguely through tears of joy and shaky legs. John whispered in my ear, "You look beautiful," and when the priest said, "You may kiss the bride," he gave me a long, loving kiss I shall always remember.

The new house was taking a lot of money and since we had to pay for everything ourselves, we kept the reception small. It was nice, though. I chose not to have a father-daughter dance although John did dance with Mindy, a wonderful scene to watch. At the end of the evening, Mindy went home with my parents and John and I went back to the townhouse and stayed up until 3:00 A.M. opening presents. The next morning we left for a weekend honeymoon at a nice hotel in Port Huron.

Despite my apprehension, at this point things were going very well. Mindy was in a new school and she loved it. I had settled into my new job and John's business was really taking off. We moved into the new, as yet, unfinished house. It had only one working plug in each room and there was still much to do to complete it, but it was ours.

One weekend when it was Bobby's turn to take Mindy, she became upset.

"Mommy, I don't want to go over there," she said.
This was the first time I had heard this from her. "Why? It's his turn."
"I just don't want to."
"There must be a reason."
"I don't like it there anymore."
"Why? What happened? Did he do something to you?"
"He has a new girlfriend and I don't like her."
"Is she mean to you?"
"Yes. She doesn't like it when I'm there."
"Well maybe she won't be around for long."
"I think he's going to marry her."
I called Bobby and told him Mindy didn't want to go over to his place.
"Whatever," was about all he said in response.
A few days later Mindy asked if she could go over to Bobby's sister's house so that she could play with her cousins. I thought that would be okay so I packed a bag and took her over there for the weekend. Within minutes of dropping her off, Bobby called.
"What the hell do you think you're doing taking Mindy to my sister's?"
"She wanted to go see her cousins."
"But you couldn't bring her over here?"
"She didn't want to go. I told you that."
"Why? What are you telling her about me? You giving her some bullshit lies?"
"If you really want to know, she doesn't like it over there anymore because of your new girlfriend."
"Is that so?"
"She says she's mean to her."
"She ain't mean she's just different than you—thank goodness."
"That's not what she says."
"Well, it's what I say."
"I'm not letting her go over there to have someone treat her badly. I had enough of that when I was growing up."
"You're going to do exactly what the judge said you have to do."
"Mistreating Mindy wasn't part of the deal. She isn't going there and that's that."

"I'll see you in court," he said slamming down the phone.

I was so upset I couldn't think straight for the rest of the day. When John came home he could see how distraught I was so I told him about the call from Bobby.

"Don't worry," he said. "If it comes to that she's old enough to speak for herself."

Well, it did come to that. I got a notice from Friend of the Court saying there would be a custody hearing in two weeks. John told me over and over that there was no way I was going to lose Mindy and although logically I knew that was so, I couldn't shake the anxious feeling. For those two weeks I was a complete emotional wreck. My emotions trumped logic and I was petrified. Had John not been there I honestly think I would have had a nervous breakdown. I was certainly on the verge of one.

"Don't worry, honey," John would say. "Just don't ask for more money. That'll just complicate things. I'm making good money now and I'll take care of you. You know that, don't you?"

"I did know that, but it didn't stop me from being a nervous wreck when I went to court knowing I'd have to face a hostile Bobby. He was already in the courtroom when I got there and he gave me a stare that let me know his intentions.

When the judge asked him why he was there, Bobby told him he had already been granted bankruptcy and had brought the papers with him so that the judge could add the child support. He said he could no longer afford the $25 a week payments.

Well I thought the judge was going to fall out of his seat.

"You can't file bankruptcy on your children! Unless you have something else for the court…"

"Your Honor, my wife…my ex wife…doesn't let our daughter see me. I mean I'm paying child support and I have some rights to see my own kid."

The judge looked at me. "What's going on?"

"No. Absolutely not," I said. "I've never told her not to see him, but she doesn't want to go over there. She says his new girlfriend is nasty to her. I think she's old enough to make up her own mind about things like this."

"That's not true, "said Bobby. "Nobody treats her bad. That's just her mother's excuse for wanting to keep her all tied up just like her mother did to her."

"If he really wants to see her he can always go to his sister's house when Mindy is over there playing with her cousins, but he never does."

This jousting went on for a while and I could see the judge was quickly getting tired of it.

"All right, that's enough. You both need to see a family counselor," the judge said ending the session.

When I got in the elevator, Bobby followed me and I spoke up to him in a way that I should have done years earlier.

"What the hell is wrong with you," I said in a voice just barely below a full- out scream. "Your daughter is happy and well-adjusted. Why do you want to turn that upside down?"

I could see the veins in his neck bulge out like when he got into one of his drinking rages. "I pay child support and I have every goddamned right to see her if I want."

"She's old enough to make her own choices."

"Well she ain't going to do that if you're telling her lies about me."

"I don't have to tell her lies. She doesn't like who you're with now and she doesn't want to be anyplace around her. That's good enough for me. I'm not going to force her to go."

"I'm her father and that damn well gives me rights."

"Well, you sure as hell don't act like one."

When the elevator door opened I rushed out feeling angry but proud. For once I had stood my ground in the face of conflict. Maybe it was the beginning of a new me. Maybe.

When I got home, I asked Mindy if she wanted to go back to seeing her dad again.

"John's my dad," she said. "I want him to adopt me."

We talked to my lawyer about that but he said it would be extremely unlikely that any judge would grant that as long as her real father was in the picture.

"But there is something else you could do," he said. "If she is willing, your daughter could change her last name to yours."

"That's better than nothing," said John.

"But you have to understand," continued the lawyer, "Your ex can still contest."

"And he probably will," I added.

"He'll have six weeks from the time you file."

Mindy thought it was a great idea, so we immediately filed the paperwork and put a legal notice in the paper.

At the scheduled date, John, Mindy, and I walked arm in arm into the courtroom. I was expecting another big scene between Bobby and me but I didn't see him anyplace in the room. All during the time the judge was asking Mindy questions about why she was doing this, I expected Bobby to come bursting in at any moment. But he never did and just like that Mindy had our name. I was proud and I know John was, too.

Later I learned that Bobby was telling everyone that Mindy wasn't really his daughter anyway. He was claiming that she was his older brother's child. I couldn't believe he was saying that. First he insisted the child he had out of wedlock wasn't his, now he was saying his daughter wasn't his.

He could spin a web of lies the likes of which I had never known. That is, until I began spinning my own.

SEVEN

✦

It seems I couldn't ever have the good without the bad.

The good part: Our marriage was great, Mindy was doing well in school, John's business was continuing to grow faster than either of us thought would ever happen, and we were talking about having a baby. The bad part: Dealing with Mother.

As addicted to the game as she already was, she was becoming even more so. My problem was that now she didn't want to go without me and I had a hard time saying no. It was putting a real strain on our marriage. Every time the phone rang in the afternoon I knew it was Mom begging me to go to Canada with her. Sometimes that meant having to choose between going with her or doing something with John. I know that should have been an easy decision to make, but it wasn't.

As I look back, I think I had a tremendous need to feel wanted by my parents and taking Mom to Bingo made me feel that way. I never got more attention from Mom than when I was playing Bingo with her. Sometimes Father even called and asked me to take her and that in its own way made me feel that Father approved of me.

As time went on, John was becoming more and more annoyed by the situation. I desperately wanted to please John. No, I desperately needed to please John and to do that I had to stop taking Mom to Bingo, but if I stopped I knew I would lose my parents' approval.

I had scores of discussions with John about this and some turned into real arguments.

"I don't like the routine you're getting into," he'd say. "You have to jump every time your mother says so, have to take her to Bingo because she wants to go. What about everybody else? Don't we matter?"

"Of course, you do."

"Well, you sure as hell don't act like it sometimes. Maybe you could tell her no once in a while."

"I know. I'll try."

"You don't have to try, just do it."

I didn't know how to tell Mom she was causing a problem at home but I think she sensed it anyway. Sometimes when she asked me to go I'd tell her I'd have to speak with John first.

"Why? Is he upset or something?" she'd ask.

I wouldn't tell her the truth because I didn't want her to have a problem with John so I'd say something like, "No, I just have to check the schedule and make sure we not committed to something else."

During almost every obligatory Sunday dinner a conversation about Bingo would come up and she'd ask me to take her when we were finished. John would give me a look somewhere between annoyance and disgust.

Obviously my relationship with my mother has always been complicated. She was very demanding in the sense that she always wanted things to be done in the way that she wanted them done. For example, she virtually demanded that we go to their house for Sunday dinner no matter what else might have been going on. I know John's parents would have liked to have us there sometimes, too, but that didn't seem to matter.

When John and I were first together we went along with this but eventually we sometimes made other weekend plans that meant we had to miss the obligatory meal. My parents were irked whenever this happened and made sure that we got the message. The only way to make up the missed dinner was to schedule another Bingo date.

Then, too, my brothers and sisters often came to me with their problems and I always tried to help them out the best I could. This also bothered Mom. She wanted to be the one they turned to, not me. Still, I couldn't turn them down. Isn't this is what a family is for—to help each other out? Mother, though, seemed to want to keep everyone in the family in a tight little bubble over which she had dominion.

John said it was a control issue and I think he was right. I could sense growing tension between John and Mom. The more successful he became with his business, the more she seemed to resent him. She was losing control of a daughter and that scared her. Maybe she saw me as a threat. I didn't see it that way, but perhaps she did.

One evening after dinner I sat down with John and told him everything about my family relationship from the time I was a child until I met him. He said that explained a lot.

"Your parents give you conditional love," he said again. "Mine never did. No matter what, I knew they were always there for me and I knew they always loved me."

I never had the opportunity to meet his dad because he died before I met John, but his mother was a wonderful woman and I envied the relationship they had.

"Remember when you said all you wanted was a house and to be a stay-at-home-mom?"

"Sure."

"Still want that?"

"Yeah. When Mindy was little I had to pay Mom $50 a week to look after her. I don't want to do that again. I want to be a full-time mother."

"Well, you've got the house. Now, how about we go to work on another baby that you can stay home with?"

A few nights later he took me by the hand and led me into the shower where we made love. Don't ask me why, but by the next day I knew we had conceived. When I missed my period, I went to the doctor's office. I had to sit for a while in the waiting area with an older woman who didn't look at all happy. Two days later I called the office and was told the test came back negative. I couldn't believe it. I felt sure I was pregnant. I even wondered if my blood work had gotten mixed up with the other woman in the office.

That weekend, Debbie came by and said we should go out and buy a pregnancy test. When we came back from the drugstore, John was working out in the garage. We went upstairs and took the test. I told my sister I didn't want to see the results as they were developing so I went downstairs and sat on the couch while she watched. When she came down with a smile on her face I knew the results were positive.

When I told John, he was so excited I thought he was going to jump out of his skin.

"But the doctor said..."

"I think they mixed up my blood with another woman's."

We told everyone and started on the baby's room right away. I wasn't sure what Mindy would think, but when I told her she said she thought it was great.

A few months into the pregnancy I started spotting a little. One day at work it seemed worse so I called my ob/gyn who said it wasn't uncommon, but to be on the safe side, I should go home and put my feet up. I left work early and on the way home the bleeding got worse. By the time I pulled into the driveway, I was scared to death because the car seat was drenched. John was working on the side of the house when I showed up, so he saw what was happening and immediately carried me up to the bathroom.

"I'll call the doctor," he said in a voice of pure panic.

I was on the toilet and the blood was just pouring out. The office told John to get to the emergency room quick and that if there was anything in the toilet, to bring it with us. Unfortunately there was. John drove like crazy.

"Don't worry, it will be okay," he said unconvincingly.

Not surprisingly, when we got to the hospital the young doctor examining me said I had a miscarriage and would need an emergency DNC. When John came in the room he looked devastated. We hugged and cried.

A little later a second doctor said the same thing but wanted an ultrasound first. During the procedure the technician began calling for a doctor to come into the room. I was scared because I didn't know what was going on. Then the nurse informed me that there was a heartbeat and that the baby's sack was intact.

"Why am I bleeding so much?" I asked her.

"I don't know," she said looking a little perplexed.

When I was back in the emergency room, John asked the nurse what was in the sack he removed from the toilet.

"Most likely your wife was carrying twins and lost one," she said.

"You mean the other one's okay?"

"For the moment, yes."

"What does that mean?"

"I'm afraid there's a chance this one won't survive either."

"What kind of a chance?"

"It's highly likely."

We were sent home where all I could do was cry and wait. I took a leave from work and went in for weekly ultrasounds. Each time I was afraid I'd hear the bad news, but each time they told me the baby's heartbeat was strong. Little by little we were becoming hopeful. By the sixth month the bleeding had stopped completely and I went back to work. Shortly after that I began running a high fever and was having difficulty taking a deep breath. When we returned to the emergency room they said I had pneumonia and admitted me. Concern replaced the hope as I was worried that this would harm the baby. I was there for five days. When I went home I was still feeling a little weak and decided not to return to work until after the baby was born.

I made sure Mindy was involved in everything—fixing up the baby's room, getting baby supplies, and everything else involved with a bringing a new baby home. She had grown into a tall, beautiful young lady and I was proud of her.

One evening when the contractions started, John wanted to rush me to the hospital, but I convinced him they weren't strong or regular enough yet. John and Mindy fell asleep on the couch while I stayed up timing the contractions. About 2:00 AM I woke them up.

"I think it's time."

They were more nervous than I was. We drove to my sister's, dropped off Mindy, and made a bee-line for the hospital. As soon as we entered the freeway we saw flashing lights behind us. John pulled the car onto the shoulder and started to get out when the police officer told him to stay right where he was.

"Do you know how fast you were going?" he asked.

"My wife's in labor," John said.

The officer took one look at me and said, "Follow me."

With the police escort we were quickly at the hospital. About 2 ½ hours later I was ready to deliver. In the delivery room I started pushing but the doctor told me to stop. The baby was bigger than they thought so the doctor said he was going to cut me. There was no time to numb me, so he just cut and I pushed. The baby came out at 8 pounds, 3 ounces. She was bald but beautiful and perfectly healthy.

When the doctor was stitching me back up John said, "Hey doctor, while you're at it, can you put an extra stitch in?"

I didn't have any idea what he meant, but John and the doctor had a good laugh.

Once home Cathy turned out to be a difficult baby. It wasn't unusual for her to cry all night long. John helped out when he could but his booming business kept him quite busy. Mindy couldn't wait to get home from school to play with her new little sister and proved to be a big help, especially when I was getting dinner ready. I talked with my doctor about her colic but he offered little advice. I experimented with different formulas and eventually resorted to soy milk which seemed to help a little.

John's business was going so well that he told me I wouldn't need to go back to work. I would be the stay-at-home mom he promised.

I went to see the owner of the company I had been working for. As soon as I walked into the office he knew what I was going to say. I started crying and told him I just couldn't leave my new daughter. He had been very good to me and it wasn't easy to leave so suddenly.

He smiled. "I know. Do you know someone who can replace you?"

I recommended another girl in the office who was happy to get the promotion.

So many people told me Cathy had the worst case of colic they had ever seen and I was exhausted most of the time. Still I couldn't help thinking about what it would have been like had both babies made it. There's a void there that I think will never completely go away.

Losing the one baby was still bothering me. I tried several times to talk to John about it but he avoided the subject and dismissed my concerns by saying that God does everything for a reason so maybe the other baby was sick. I started rationalizing that maybe I lost the other baby so that Cathy would survive.

When she was two a very strange thing happened. Cathy came up to me and said, "Mommy, where is my brother?"

I was absolutely dumbfounded by the question. Where could she have come up with the idea? I checked with John and Mom and just about everybody else. No one had said a word to her about a brother lost before birth.

I never talked with her about this and she never mentioned it again. I can only conclude that when babies are in the womb they are aware of things and the trauma of truth eases the memory of being in the womb.

After a few months of dealing with sleepless colic-filled nights,

John thought we all needed a vacation so we arranged to rent a cottage in the sand dunes for a week. The first night there Cathy cried all night. The next night without me knowing about it, John took her for a long ride on the dunes. He had built up a Chevy pickup with big tires and a powerful engine that he could use to dash up and down the dunes, sometimes at scary angles. Cathy was in a car seat and apparently fell asleep for the entire ride. When I found out I was furious. It would have been easy to flip over on the soft sand.

"Don't worry," John said. "I was careful."

"I don't care. That was just stupid."

"Besides, she's never slept longer in her life."

Despite the scare and the long crying spells, it was a wonderful week. John and Mindy spent a lot of time together on the dunes. He even let her drive a little which thrilled her no end.

When we got back home, the calls from Mom started again and I was feeling the pressure from John.

"Honey, you just can't keep doing this," he said in another one of our long conversations about Bingo and Mom.

"I know."

"Then just stop. Tell her no. It's that easy."

"It's not, though."

"Be strong."

"How about I tell her I'll go with her 2 times a week and that's all?"

"How about no times."

"It's a compromise—2 times."

"You've got a husband, a young baby, a girl who needs you here…"

"And a mother."

It wasn't long before the two-night-a-week Bingo arrangement had become three and sometimes four. Almost every night during dinner she would call and beg me to go and John was losing patience. He'd usually give in, but his resentment towards my mom was showing and she knew it. She responded accordingly and the tension between the two escalated.

I didn't know what to do. On the surface it would appear that the solution was simple: I had a good marriage and two wonderful children, so just ignore my mother. I loved my husband, so what was the problem? It wasn't that simple, though. I liked the attention I was getting from my mom, and despite my protestations, I liked playing.

When Cathy began going to pre-school I came up with a plan. I would take Mom to Bingo while Cathy was at school and then I would be home in the evening. This worked for about two weeks and then Mom pressured me to play at times when Cathy wasn't at school. I knew this was getting out of hand but I didn't know how to stop it.

One day while I was cooking, John came into the kitchen with a very determined look on his face.

"I've had enough," he said.

"What do you mean?"

"Pick one: Bingo or me."

"What?"

"It's your choice. You can have a real life with your husband or you can have a life playing Bingo with your mother. Not both. Choose."

Obviously making the right choices wasn't something I'd always been good at but I was pretty sure about this one.

I assured John that I would forevermore choose him over anything or anybody else.

He hugged me, and probably for the first time in his life, actually cried.

I knew I would have to break the news to Mom and that wasn't going to be easy. I know it should have been. I know I should have done it a long time ago but I couldn't bring myself to do it.

The next day she called and rather than tell her the truth, I came up with an excuse. Then the next day, another one. Each time she called, I came up with a lie and learned that a lie is often easier to deal with than the truth. Certainly it is for a coward. Toothaches, doctor's visits, flat tires, teacher's meetings, and anything reasonable were grist for the excuse mill. First she was disappointed, then annoyed, then angry, and then the calls stopped. She was clearly upset and that bothered me but losing John would have bothered me more.

With Thanksgiving around the corner, I called her to ask what to bring for dinner. She was usually chatty with me but this time all I got was an icy, "Salad if you want."

"Anything else?"

"Nope."

I was terribly hurt by this. Her anger gnawed at me like a dull pain that never let up. I would have done anything short of fighting with John about it to make it go away. Mother knew exactly what she was doing—making me pay for ignoring her.

Mother was always the instigator for our Bingo trips, but it wasn't that I didn't enjoy them, too. So after not playing for a time, I got the itch again. One night I asked John if he would go with me. I didn't think he'd object to the game itself just so long as I didn't take off with Mother and leave him with Cathy.

"No, I don't think so."

"Oh, come on, it will be fun."

"I've got things to do."

"You always have things to do."

"All of which sound like more fun than sitting with a bunch of women waiting for the right ball to come up."

"You'd be surprised. You've got to really stay alert, particularly if you're playing a lot of cards."

"You're right about one thing. I would be surprised if it were fun."

After he turned me down a few times, I resorted to cajoling and finally begging. I think he eventually came to the conclusion that the urge was building within me and that if I didn't go with him, I'd end up going with Mom again. He probably saw going with me as the lesser of two evils.

When we got to the game, I had to explain everything to him—the rules, procedures, etiquette.

"Maybe you shouldn't play with too many cards at first. Sometimes it's hard to find all the numbers quickly enough if you haven't played a lot."

"Oh, you don't think I'm smart enough to play Bingo?"

"You'll see. It's not as easy as you think."

Well naturally John picked up the game quickly. He said he enjoyed it but I know he was just saying that for my sake. Still, I liked playing with him and I appreciated the fact that he cared enough that he wanted to satisfy me.

A couple of years went by and my relationship with my parents was continuously deteriorating. I felt the tension at every family event. Mother was punishing me. It was uncomfortable enough that John and I were always the first to leave and my sister would tell me we were invariably the subject of conversation the minute the door closed. This upset me greatly but I wasn't going to lose John. One of my sisters took over the role of taking Mom to Bingo, but she couldn't go as often as I had been able to, so Mom went back to going by herself to local halls.

For a long time I had told myself that while I enjoyed playing Bingo, it was only for Mother's sake that I played. I was sacrificing to please her. I was lying to myself.

I was addicted. People can be addicted to all sorts of things—drugs, alcohol, shoplifting, smoking, television, even chocolate. I was becoming addicted to gambling. Lots of people can eat a chocolate bar and not become addicted to chocolate, just as lots of people can play Bingo and not get addicted to it. They can play a game or two, enjoy the experience and happily walk away maybe to play another day or maybe not. For one reason or another, some people, including me, play and can't stop. Why this is so I can't say for sure.

I know I don't have good stress management skills. I've been told this may have something to do with it. A lack of self-confidence and the need to seek the approval of others is probably also involved. Growing up I always felt this need and I think it stayed with me for a long time.

My Bingo obsession was roiling within me but things were about to get worse—much worse. One day I read in the paper that they put slot machines in the casinos on the Canadian side of the river.

EIGHT

✦

The casino in Canada was on a riverboat. I talked John into taking me and the first time we walked in I was immediately captivated by the mix of sounds and sparkling lights. It was all high energy and it was beautiful, like a magical world far removed from the drudgery of Detroit.

For a while we watched people playing. We observed how they handled their money, pushed the buttons, sat with excited expectations as the magical wheels spun and spun. Then we found unused machines next to each other and I began my slot machine compulsion. It all seemed, harmless and engaging, innocent and simple enough.

We started going about once a month—me enthusiastically, John reluctantly. He often pretended to be having a good time for my sake, but in reality, most of the time he was bored. He would much rather have been out in the wilds hunting deer or fishing in an icy stream. A beautiful fall morning in the woods held appeal to him; a smoke-filled room with loud machines didn't. Any time he won (once he won $1,000) he wanted to pocket the winnings and go home. I always wanted to stay and play more.

Once a month wasn't enough for me, but it was more than enough for John. He was getting busier and busier at work and when he had any time off, the lure of the outdoors always beckoned. But I cajoled and pressed him to go more often. Deep down I knew it was wrong but the urge was overwhelming.

Everybody knew the economy in Detroit was lousy and getting worse. The auto makers were losing money, mostly because of the Japanese cars, and stories about layoffs were in the news practically every day. Then the voters in the state said it was okay to put three casinos in Detroit.

Stories about the progress of the casinos promising a bright new future for the city were constantly in the papers.

"Roulette wheels, slot machines and greeters in skimpy swimsuits are welcoming gamblers to Detroit's first casino," said the Detroit Free Press.

"The $225 million MGM Grand, inside a converted Internal Revenue Service building, is the first and largest of three casinos scheduled to open in Detroit over the next few weeks."

Glitzy brochures made them seem like heaven on earth.

"Your winning streak begins at MGM Grand Detroit. Step onto the gaming floor and discover all the comforts you can handle while playing slots and video poker. Pull in all the excitement with over 4,000 of the latest and greatest slots and video poker! Take a spin on all your classic favorites, or touch up on our multi-line video slots, ranging from 1 cent to $100! And MGM Grand Detroit always has the newest themes, with big payouts, exciting bonuses and huge progressive jackpots! For the hottest slots around and the newest games in town, MGM Grand Detroit is always on top of the game!"

Right from the start the casinos did well, taking in billions of dollars. From what the papers said, they were exactly what Detroit needed and lots of other cities were jealous. Of course, the money had to come from someplace, so the racetracks, and the state lottery were losing customers, and some businesses like restaurants were saying the casinos were taking away customers who would rather gamble than spend money on eating out. Of course, the casinos were employing lots of people to work there so that had to be good for Detroit, too.

I didn't really care about any of that, though. All I knew is that we had places near where I lived where I could go and play the machines and still get home quickly enough that it wouldn't look too suspicious.

At first they opened temporary casinos, but then they built new ones that were big, beautiful, and very appealing. They had all the flashiness and glamour I had seen in the pictures of Las Vegas casinos. They were bright, clean, exciting, and to some of us, impossible to ignore. The MGM Grand had their 4,500 shiny, beckoning machines set up in row after row. Even if someone was looking for you it might take a while in the maze of colorful machines. You could be among hundreds or thousands of people but still feel you were in your own world with your machine.

In case the machines at the MGM weren't treating you well, you could always go over to the Greektown Casino.

"Greektown Casino's slots and video poker machines are second-to-none! You'll find all your favorites among our over 2,600 slot machines, plus we scour the country to give you the newest, most cutting-edge machines around. Plus we've added 25,000 more square feet of pure slot-filled gaming space. That means you can spend more time having fun and less time waiting for a machine!

Our slots come in every denomination your heart desires: penny, two cents, nickel, quarter, fifty cents, on up to fifty- and hundred-dollar machines. Want to get *really* lucky? Our large selection of In-house and Wide Area Progressives are linked to other machines within Greektown Casino or with other casinos in the market. This offers the value of a larger jackpot for the same price!

So visit us today...there's thousands of slots to play!"

The Motor City Casino advertised, "Each slot chair is fully adjustable and ergonomically designed for comfort and ease of movement. With over 2,500 games to choose from, you'll be sure to find a favorite."

To me, it was like Christmas every day, a virtual Disneyland for adults.

It didn't take long before I was hooked and took my place on the dishonorable roll of the other 3 million compulsive gamblers who live in the United States.

I began a period in my life during which, I'm embarrassed to say, not even John, my daughters, my parents, or my conscience would come before my insatiable thirst to play the slot machines.

The urge to gamble, how does one explain it? You can't. You either have it or you don't. Every morning I'd wake up and think about playing. Every night if I hadn't played I lamented the lost day. The spinning wheels were becoming the focus of my life, a fact I denied to everyone but myself.

John knew he'd have to take me occasionally if I were to quench my thirst for the machines and back off on the begging. He was always reluctant but he thought that if I went occasionally it would satisfy me. It didn't.

The more I pushed him to go, the more concerned he became. He'd find excuses not to go too often just as I had with Mom and Bingo. He'd work late, find projects around the house that had to be done, work on his truck. By this time in our lives we were financially secure and making more money than I ever imagined I would have. As time when on I realized that if I gave him good sex, he would be more likely to take me to a casino.

One night coming back from playing the machines for a few hours he said,

"You've got to promise me you'll never go to a casino without me."

I know he could see the urge building in me. "You play too often as it is," he said. "You know that, don't you?"

"I wouldn't go without you. Don't worry," I said.

"Promise me that."

"Sure. I promise."

When I said that I think I really meant it, but it wasn't long before the lies started. I felt I had to play more often than we were doing together so while Cathy was at school, I'd head for a casino.

"How'd your day go, honey?" John would ask when he got home.

"Nothing special—laundry, shopping. Boring housework stuff."

"How'd your day go, honey?"

"A little gardening. That's about it."

"How'd your day go, honey?"

"Oh, I went out for coffee with one of the girls from my old office."

It didn't take long before the lies were a part of me and me of them but I couldn't tell which part. Lies, lies, and more lies. I had lists of them. I was shopping. I ran out of gas. I was at a movie.

If John was around when I went to the casino I would usually use the shopping story. Often I would go when I knew he was working on a big job and wouldn't be home until late. Sometimes I would even stop at a store and buy something to prove that I was shopping. I'm not sure he always believed me, but as long as I was getting away with it, I didn't care.

Naturally the gambling took money but since I was taking care of the household and some of the business finances, I soon learned how to sneak money out of various accounts. John was too busy working and attracting new clients to notice. As fast as he was putting on new workers and lining up new accounts I was siphoning off the profits. Of course, I always told myself that I'd replace the money with my winnings. I was only "borrowing" funds until I hit the jackpot.

"How'd your day go, honey?"

"Lousy. I had a dentist appointment."

Since he was so busy with the business it was easy for me to say we needed more for this or that when in reality all I really needed was more cash for the insatiable machines. I had credit cards with good credit limits and the bills came to me. I knew I could stretch out the playing seemingly forever. Just so long as John was making it, I could find a place to put it—temporarily. Payback was only a win away.

The inside of a casino was bright, exciting, promised so much more as the nights wore on, and no matter how long you played the lights always glistened. The row after row of chrome and lacquer machines call out to you as you stroll seductively by—play me, sweetheart, I'll be good to you. I promise to be your one and only true love tonight. There are scores of these machines, all making the same promise—Neptune's Treasure, the Fabulous Fifties, Black Gold, Lucky 7's, Stars and Bars, and oh, so many more. Enticement and seduction is their business and they're very good at it.

The minute I walked into the slot area I felt as if I were wrapped in a protective cocoon. I didn't have to answer to anyone and no one criticized me. I was simply an anonymous player like all the other anonymous players. I felt like the machines loved me. Of course it's absurd, but more than once I could have sworn a machine winked at me.

This was my not-so-secret, secret place, my safe place. Just so long as I won back the money I'd lost, all would be right with the world. I felt in control, accepted. Deep down I probably knew it was an illusion but I wasn't about to ignore or challenge it.

Most of my days were either spent thinking about gambling or thinking about what lies I could come up with so that I could gamble. John was becoming suspicious but I was getting better at the lying than I was the gambling. As I came to learn, it isn't a very big step from compulsive gambling to chronic lying. I buried my conscience beneath the last quarter in the bottom of my purse.

Gambling became my life. I would wake in the morning and the first thing I thought about was how I could get to a casino without raising any red flags to John or my family. I lined up the lies like strings of beads that I picked off one at a time as needed.

When driving to the casino there was always a sense of excitement but it came with a tinge of dread that John might call me. If only cell phones hadn't been invented yet. When I got to the casino I rushed into the gaming area and got two Diet Pepsis with cherries and headed right to my favorite nickel machines. If I was winning or just breaking even I would usually move on to the $1 machines. I would start out playing machines that you could win double or triple the amount if that specific symbol (double/triple) on the machine would line up with sevens, bars, cherries, etc. Then I would usually go on to the "Blazing Sevens" progressive jackpot. These machines doled out at $1,000 if you got three blazing sevens in a row. It wasn't hard to lose a lot of money on these machines and usually I did. I would get frustrated but I would still go and get more money out of the ATM machine in an attempt to win the money back. It's hard to leave a machine when you know that you have put a lot of money into it. After the Blazing Sevens if I had time I would go back to the nickel machines thinking people had put a lot of money in the machines they would be ready to pay off.

A common thread among slot players is the theory that when a machine hasn't paid off for some time, it is due. You can never know when a machine will hit, but every player believes that machines that are overdue will sooner or later pay off big. So when someone plays a machine without winning for a long time and then leaves it, others will jump on the chance to play that machine because obviously it's overdue for a big payoff. Now I know the odds of hitting any particular combination are the same on every play. If a machine is programmed to pay out its top jackpot, on the average once every 10,000 plays, your chances of hitting it are one in 10,000 on any given button push. If you've been standing there for days and have played 10,000 times, the odds on the next play will still be one in 10,000. Those odds are long-term averages. In the short term, the machine could go 100,000 plays without letting loose of the big one, or it could pay it out twice in a row. But this is not the way most of us played. We looked for those machines which we were absolutely sure were about to pay off big.

Sometimes I'd get furious when I'd play a machine for a long time without winning, only to watch someone else win big on that machine after I left it. A sour taste would coat my mouth.

Another vague theory among slot players (and that's all I ever played) is that there are "loose" machines and "tight" machines and that playing the "loose" machines is always better because it has something to do with the average returns they paid out. So looking for "loose" machines was part of the playing experience. Now it's not exactly like the casinos put signs on the loose machines saying "play me and you'll have the best chance of winning big," but lots of players think they know where to find them. This is so, despite the fact that it is supposedly the biggest secret in the casino industry. Probably more secrets have been pried out of the CIA than from casino executives about where they put the "loose" machines.

One explanation I heard was that they were always at the slot crosswalks where lots of people could see players there and so act as a lure to draw others to the machines. They are never in the middle of a row where fewer people can see them. Nothing excites slot players more than hearing someone at a slot crosswalk screaming with joy as coins cascade into the hopper. It keeps them playing, too. I don't know if this is true or not, but it's what a lot of players think.

As soon as I neared the banks of machines I could feel my pulse quicken with a mix of exhilaration, excitement, even danger. I could easily lose myself here, a condition I looked forward to. Mostly I stayed with the machines I knew how to play well. I'd sit at a machine, my face expressionless, my mind nearly blank in a trance-like state of desirable non-existence. The world with all its problems was turning someplace outside the casino but I didn't have to care about that.

I would stay until I was pushing the clock or knew that John would start wondering where I was. When John would go to the Upper Peninsula I would go to the casinos a lot more—sometimes twice a day, depending on what was going on at home. If my daughter was spending the night at a friend's house I would stay at the casino until 3:00 or 4:00 in the morning. That of course would depend on whether I was winning or had maxed out the cash advances for the day.

When I sat in front of those machines I lost all track of time but I constantly checked my cell phone to see if John had tried to call. If he had I would leave the noisy casino and go to my car to call him so he would think I was on the road running errands. If I thought he doubted my story I would leave the casino and go home worrying all the way about how I would convince him that I wasn't gambling. Guilt constantly gnawed at me like a piranha on a carcass. Gambling had such a choke hold on me that I was living two distinct lives: the careful housewife/mother, and the risk-taking compulsive/secretive gambler.

I didn't talk much to the other gamblers at the casinos but after a while I started recognizing some of those who seemed always to be there. We were like a silent tacit club of those who knew what each one of us was going through—the compulsion, the frustration, the anger, the occasional moments of joy. Often we'd put so much money into a machine without winning, that we'd ask one of the others to watch our machine while we went to get more money since it would soon be time for the machine to pay out.

I don't know how many times I told myself that quitting shouldn't be hard--another lie. Sometimes I'd really try; other times I'd just give in to the impulse, trying to convince myself that it didn't really matter because I didn't have a gambling problem. I'd try to convince myself that I could stop anytime I needed to.

The reality was that even though I was overwhelmed by my money losses and despondent over my loss of control, I couldn't stop gambling. I know it seems like it ought to be "wouldn't" not "couldn't" but I couldn't. Every day I fought the urge to gamble and on most days the battle was lost. When the casinos beckoned with the promise of an adrenaline rush, I answered and then, like so many gamblers, when I lost big, I "chased." I had to win back my losses. Sooner or later I would hit a big jackpot and then I would quit.

Here's a question I've asked myself a zillion times without ever coming up with a reasonable answer: What is it that turns someone who can gamble for an hour or so and then walk away, into someone who can't? I simply don't know. Why does the fat lady continue to eat the sundae knowing it will only make her bigger? Why does the drinker continue to down the whiskey knowing his liver is giving out? Someone may know the answers, but I certainly don't.

John is certainly no fool and it didn't take him long to figure out that I was gambling without him—a lot. We had a couple of short confrontations about this and then some that weren't so short.

"You're distracted and you're nervous. I know the signs, you're gambling again, aren't you?"

"No, I'm not."

"You're preoccupied. It's like your mind is someplace else. You get upset so easily. That's what happens when you've been gambling."

My anxiety level went sky high every time John walked in the door. Anxiety was my constant companion and it often it gave me headaches and a constricted chest. Sometimes I became weak and nauseated and I could feel the acid rising in my throat.

I convinced myself that if I had to I could live with John hating me, but losing respect for me was a whole different matter and I knew that was inevitable. I was worried sick all the time, a frantic, emotional wreck. But still I gambled.

I'd like to be able to say that love, or caring, or something else as noble was the dominant emotion in my life, but the reality is it was guilt, plain and simple and guilt makes joy impossible. I was joyless, deflated, empty, as lost as a woman could possibly be. I hated myself.

I worried all the time. I worried about the money I was losing. I worried about John finding out how much I was playing. I worried about what I had become. I was tense and I was depressed and I was angry at other players when they won. Still, I couldn't stop. That's how addicted I was.

Showdowns with John were becoming as regular as the sunrise.

"You went to the casino yesterday, didn't you?"

"I was at my sister's." I knew she'd cover for me so this was always a handy lie.

"Barbara, I know you did. You were at the Grand."

"Honest, I wasn't."

It's a terrible thing to live a lie, but that's exactly what I'd sunk to. One evening he came home from work and stormed into the kitchen.

"Okay now I know damn well you were at the casino this afternoon."

"No, I wasn't."

"How can you lie to me like that?"

I turned back to the cake I was mixing so I wouldn't have to look at him. "I had like a zillion errands, that's all."

"You saying you weren't at the casino?"

"Absolutely not."

"Barbara, this has got to stop."

"What are you talking about?"

"You know damn well what I'm talking about—the gambling, the lying. It's out of control. You're out of control. Can't you see that? You're destroying everything that we've built up."

"I swear to you I wasn't gambling today."

"Well then, something is seriously wrong with me because I know you were at the Grand all damn afternoon. Want to know how I know? I saw you, that's how I know. I saw your SUV heading downtown and I followed you right to the entrance of the Grand's parking structure."

"You couldn't have because I wasn't even there. Lots of SUVs look the same. Lots of them look like mine."

"It was you, Barbara."

"I know you think you're always right about these things, but this time you've got it wrong. You followed the wrong person."

"Enough!"

"I know you think…"

"What's happening to you? I don't know you anymore. You've turned into a monster. The gambling is bad enough, but the lying on top of it?"

"Don't you trust me anymore?"

"I can't. You make up these bullshit stories and then lie through your teeth about them. Or are you so screwed up that you can't tell the truth from a lie anymore? Are you? Are you that far gone?"

"Why can't you just trust me?"

"Are you kidding? Trust you? Every time I turn my back…"

"You think you know everything but you don't."

"Really? Well I know this: I know you're not the person I married."

"Well then, maybe you married the wrong person."

"Maybe I did."

John, of course was right about everything he was saying and I knew it, but I wouldn't or couldn't admit it. Telling lies to cover my gambling addiction had become more than a habit. It had become second nature, a way of life. Not only could I bend the truth with great conviction, but I took great comfort in it whereas telling the truth was difficult and uncomfortable. I know now that like other things that provide escape from discomfort such as alcohol and drugs, lying can become addictive and very hard to stop.

John popped open a beer and was downing it like a madman. I'd never seen him this angry before. "It's got to stop right now," he said between gulps.

"Or what?"

"You know damn well, or what."

By this time I had resorted to my usual crying routine. I was completely humiliated because he had not only caught me gambling, he also caught my lying, and I had no way out except to do what I had frequently done before—escape. I ran upstairs. "I'm not going to listen to this anymore," I cried. "If you can't believe that I'm not gambling, then I'm not staying here any longer."

John watched silently as I threw some things into a small suitcase.

"I'm going to Mindy's" I said.

A few years earlier, at John's surprise 40th birthday party, Mindy met a very nice hard-working tile setter. They started dating and then got married. At the time I moved in with her, she had two boys, she was running a daycare facility out of her home and was taking care of lots of children. The last thing she needed was another one hanging around—me. And a very upset one at that. I was a nervous wreck all the time. I loved John and turning my back on him like I did, tore me up. So I did what I knew to do to try to forget about it for a while—I went to the casinos.

I dragged out all of my old alibis to explain where I was going.

"I'm going to the mall to do some shopping for a few hours. Be back this evening."

"Mom, you're not going to the casino, are you?"

"No, of course not. I need some new jeans and you know how picky I am so it'll probably take a while. I'll see you later."

One afternoon I was playing a Lucky 7 machine in the middle of a row of otherwise silent and vacant machines. It wasn't very busy and I was having a particularly unprofitable time of it. Because I was still so upset, my concentration wasn't what it normally was. At one point I turned away from the machine for a moment and saw John and Cathy standing side by side at the end of the aisle.

My heart felt like it had jumped into my throat. They were looking at me with a mixture of shame and anger. I started shaking. Not only had I alienated John, but now I was sure my daughter despised me as well. That's how far down the ladder of self-pity I had descended.

Obviously there was no lie that could extricate me from this situation. I froze with them looking at me for what seemed like an eternity. No conversation was necessary.

All I heard was John saying to Cathy, "I told you."

When I could move again, I left the casino, drove back to Mindy's house, packed my things before she returned, and drove to a hotel where I checked in using cash and a false name. I was in hiding like an Al-Qaeda terrorist and didn't want John, Mindy or anyone else, for that matter, to find me. I was far too humiliated to face them. I felt like an utter and complete failure, a loser of a wife and mother who had let down everyone who had loved her. I certainly wasn't worthy of their respect and I was much too embarrassed to ask for it.

I turned off my cell phone and went into total hibernation. For two days I talked to no one. I was depressed, ashamed, and alone. I know self-esteem has always been an issue for me but now it had sunk to an all-time low.

When I finally got up the courage to call Mindy she said, "Mom, we understand you have a gambling problem. We want to help you. We love you. You need to know that. Please, let us help."

Although it seems obvious that I needed help, it was hard to admit it. My self-defense mechanism and my penchant for lying always came to the fore in situations like this. So I told her I didn't need help. How absurd this must have sounded. Eventually she convinced me to take a call from John and try to work things out, or at the very least, go back to her house.

When John called, the first thing he asked was, "Where are you?"

"I'm safe," I said.

"That's not an answer."

"I'm safe. I'm fine."

"You're not fine. I need to talk with you."

"I'm listening."

"Face to face."

"You can say whatever you need to say on the phone."

"You're not going to tell me where you are?"

"No."

"Barbara, look we need to get through this, get on with our lives in a reasonable way, and that means you've got to face the truth. You need help."

Face the truth? That's the last thing in the world I wanted to do. The truth was ugly and it hurt. And I was still angry, probably more because I was caught than because I was gambling.

"There are places to get help," he said. "There are lots of other people in the same situation who've gotten the help they've needed and now they're fine. Tell me where you are and I'll come over and meet you. We'll talk about it. I promise I won't force you to do anything you don't want to do. I just want to talk."

The thought of having to admit everything I'd tried so long and hard to hide made me sick to my stomach and the thought of having to confront John made me a complete emotional wreck. How did it all come to this? When did I go from being a casual gambler to a compulsive gambler? It's an unanswerable question. There was no one point, no one defining moment, just a slow slide into my own tangled web of lies and denials.

John worked hard to try to convince me to tell him where I was so that we could have a conversation between a caring husband and a troubled wife. Eventually I agreed and told him.

Waiting for him to show up was pure torture. I knew I needed him and at the same time I felt so guilty and vulnerable that the thought of him standing in front of me terrified me.

When he arrived he was so calm and comforting that for the first time I acknowledged what was obvious to everyone else but me—I did need help with a serious problem.

"There's an organization called Gamblers Anonymous," he said. "I've checked into it a little. They work with people who admit that they are powerless over their gambling problem, that their lives have become unmanageable. Honey, that's you, isn't it."

It was, and I know how fortunate I was to have someone like John who cared enough to try to help me through this, still it was a hard thing to face. After a lot of talking, I finally agreed to return home and try the GA program. I wasn't at all sure about this, but I was sure I couldn't spend the rest of my life living in a hotel room.

"That's the hard part," John said. "Admitting you need help. The rest will be easy."

I went home and found out there was a GA meeting at a local Salvation Army Hall. I felt uneasy about going because I suspected I was going to have to stand up in front of everyone and talk about my gambling, but I knew I had to do something and I had promised John. Mindy agreed to go with me. When we got to the hall we were directed to go downstairs to a room in which they had pushed all the tables together into one big square so that everyone would have a view of everyone else.

"Are you new here?" a woman asked as we took the seats closet to the door.

"Yes," I said.

"Nice to have you. Let me get you some paperwork to look at. Some things about our program and what you can expect."

It was a cluttered, busy room and people were wandering in and taking seats as the woman returned with the papers. She had one set for me and one for Mindy.

"No, that's all right," I said. "This is my daughter and she's just here for moral support."

"Okay, honey. We'll get started in a few minutes."

As we were waiting for the meeting to start I scanned the paperwork. "Most of us have been unwilling to admit we were real problem gamblers. No one likes to think they are different from their fellows. Therefore, it is not surprising that our gambling careers have been characterized by countless vain attempts to prove we could gamble like other people. The idea that somehow, some day, we will control our gambling is the great obsession of every compulsive gambler. The persistence of this illusion is astonishing. Many pursue it into the gates of prison, insanity or death."

According to what I read, they had a 12 step program "fundamentally based on ancient spiritual principles." I guess it was something like what I'd heard Alcoholics Anonymous uses.

1. Admit we are powerless over gambling— that our lives have become unmanageable.

2. Understand that a Power greater than ourselves can restore us to a normal way of thinking and living.

3. Decide to turn our will and our lives over to the care of this Power.

4. Make a searching and fearless moral and financial inventory of ourselves.

5. Admit to ourselves and to another human being the exact nature of our wrongs.

6. Agree we are ready to have these defects of character removed.

7. Humbly ask God to remove our shortcomings.

8. Make a list of all persons we have harmed and be willing to make amends to them all.

9. Make direct amends to such people wherever possible, except when to do so would injure them or others.

10. Continue to take personal inventory and when we are wrong, promptly admit it.

11. Seek through prayer and meditation to improve our conscious contact with God as we understood Him, praying only for knowledge of His will for us and the power to carry that out.

12. Having made an effort to practice these principles in all our affairs, try to carry this message to other compulsive gamblers.

There were maybe a dozen people around the table including us when a chubby man stood up and said, I think for our benefit, that he would be leading the meeting that night. He started going around the table and asking each person to talk about why they were there and to talk a little about their gambling problem. He also made a point to ask each person how long it had been since they had gambled.

"Hello, I'm Jack and I'm a compulsive gambler."

We sat and listened to the stories, some more interesting than others. Whenever a person said they had stopped but then gone back to gambling recently, the man who ran the meeting just said, "Don't worry about that. Today is another day. Just start all over again." As this continued, my nervousness about having to talk was giving way to annoyance. I had hoped the meeting would offer good solid information on how to stop. Instead all I was hearing were stories of people failing to quit gambling and then being told it was okay because all they needed to do was to start over again.

When it came time for me to speak, I kept my story brief but told how I started with Bingo at the church with my mom and then moved on the playing the slots.

After all the stories were done the leader asked if there was anything anyone wanted to talk about that was bothering them. There was, but it was always the same thing: How they had failed.

"It's okay. Today is a new day. Just start over again," the leader kept repeating. "You need to be proud of yourself for trying to quit. It's not easy. You should be proud."

After this went on for some time, the moderator said it was time for a prayer, so everyone bowed their heads while he read one.

As the meeting ended and people were starting to leave, one of the women who had told her story about all the times she had slipped up, came up to me and said she would like to be my sponsor and that I could call her anytime I got the urge. We exchanged phone numbers but I never called her and she never called me.

As we were leaving, Mindy said, "I don't think this is for you, Mom."

She was right. I thought the meeting was nothing but a pity party and I never went back.

While I may have admitted I needed to deal with a problem and thereby was on the road to salvation, the reality was completely different. I was lying to everyone, including myself. The lure of gambling had me and wasn't going to give up that easily. The urge always hovered and it was a constant battle to keep it at bay. Most of the battles were lost.

The compelling lure of the slot machines bore down on me like a runaway locomotive. At every opportunity I could make, or find, I headed to the casinos.

My relationship with John was deteriorating faster than I could patch it up with lies, half truths, diversions, and double-talk. I made promise after promise, some honestly put forth, few realized. "Why are you doing this to me?" John would yell and I would back-pedal trying to defend myself while absorbing as much of the punishment as he could throw.   No matter what I said, I knew I deserved it.

"What's it going to take to get you to stop this?" he'd shout. "You've got to get a handle on this."

"I swear, I'll never do it again." And I didn't...for two whole days. Then I raced back to the MGM like Richard Petty on the last lap.

Again and again, the same pattern—accusations, denials, promises, relapses, recrimination.

"Barbara, I love you," he'd say. "But you have a problem. A serious problem.   You know that, don't you?   In your heart you know that. You've got to get help."

"I know. I will."

Nothing worked for long.

John tried every strategy he could think of— pleading, ignoring, yelling.   He was like a frustrated caged animal, who with every trip I made to the casinos, was getting closer and closer to giving up.

"I'm telling you, this is your last chance," he said on more than one occasion.   "I can't continue to live like this.   Hit the machines again and I'm gone.   I can't jeopardize our future, the kids' future any longer.   I can't deal with your destructive behavior.   I won't stand for it anymore."

He was at the point where he no longer believed my promises, so I pretty much stopped offering them.   I could see the inevitable result of this, but even that couldn't stop me.

Then one day I found a receipt for a visit to a lawyer that he had neglected to put away.   It didn't take me long to find out that he had contacted the lawyer to begin divorce proceedings.   To make his point, he had planned to have me served with the papers while I was sitting in front of a machine at the MGM casino.   He figured that potential embarrassment would motivate me.   He was right.

First I panicked, and then I begged him to believe me when I said I would take a big step towards recovery.

I had heard about a program where you could go to any casino and sign yourself out. This meant that you agreed never to gamble there and they agreed never to let you. Although he was skeptical, and had every right to be, he agreed to take me to the three Detroit casinos for this purpose. The deal was that we would go to each casino, do a little gambling for the last time with John there so I didn't go overboard, and then sign out, never to return. First we went to the Motor City Casino where I signed out without playing. Then we went to the MGM Grand where we did play a little before John got impatient and I signed out there, also.

At the Greektown Casino we were told that they didn't have a sign out procedure, but that the state did have a self-exclusion program. A casino representative said he'd go and find the paperwork for me which he eventually did.

"Fill it out completely," he said "and send it in to the address on top and then you'll be signed out in all three casinos."

I promised John I would and even pretended to fill it out and mail it in. Within days I was back gambling and within a couple of weeks he had it figured out again.

"This is the last time I'm going to tell you," he said. "It's me or the machines. You choose." Having said this for the umpteenth time, he turned and walked out to the garage to work on the truck. I believed him.

The next day, I called my friend Denise and asked her if she would go with me to the State Gaming Board in downtown Detroit where I would voluntarily put myself on the self exclusion list.

September 30, 2003, Detroit, Michigan

I'm driving to Cadillac Place on West Grand in downtown Detroit with my best friend, Denise. I am excited and nervous at the same time. I'm not sure exactly what to expect. We are smoking.

This is a big step for me and I'm glad I have a friend along for support. *"I have to do this" I say reassuringly.*

"Of course you do. It's absolutely the right thing."

We park in a pay lot, go into the building, and look at the directory.

"There it is," Denise said. "Suite L-700."

The elevator is crowed but silent. When we get off and go into the office. We're the only ones there.

In a few minutes I'm talking to a man who acts like he's done this a million times before.

"You understand that if you sign this list you'll be on it for the rest of your life. You understand that, right?"

"Yes."

"You can't change your mind later."

"I know that."

"It's a lifetime ban."

"Yeah."

"And you acknowledge that you're signing of your own volition?"

"I want to do it."

"Okay then. I need you to sit down over there and read the entire document. When you're done come back to me."

"I will."

"I'll need to photograph and fingerprint you."

"Okay."

"Sign when you're absolutely sure."

I read through everything they give me. Nothing is a surprise. I knew exactly what I am getting into by coming here.

When I sign it means that for the rest of my life I can never again legally enter any casino in the state of Michigan. I will have voluntarily had myself banned.

I am reading carefully. I have to sign a statement saying that I believe I am a problem gambler and am seeking treatment. It's called the Disassociated Persons List—an exclusive list of the most screwed up gamblers in a state full of gamblers, screwed up and otherwise.

The material says my name and picture will be distributed to the Michigan Gaming Control Board, the Attorney General, the state police, and every casino in the state.

The casinos will then give my name and picture to the general managers of each casino, all managerial employees who have responsibility for casino operations, and all security and surveillance personnel. In other words my name and picture will be splattered all over the casinos. So the minute I take one step through a casino door, they're going to know I'm there and kick me out. Since I can't seem to kick myself out, I'm agreeing to let them do it for me.

What I'm really saying is I'm not strong enough to do what the state can. It's a pathetic position I know, but it's come to that. I have no self respect left. I've surrendered all dignity to the great state of Michigan.

The document I'm reading clearly says that if I'm spotted in a casino, I'll be immediately "removed from the casino premises" and a report will be sent to the "prosecutor for the county in which the casino is located."

Well, that should do it.

Even in the unlikely event that I did manage to sneak into a casino unnoticed—maybe in a disguise or something—they aren't allowed to give me any kind of credit, or let me cash a check. If they do, I don't know who'd get in more trouble—me or the casino.

Oh, yes, there's one other interesting part to the list. It says that if I am ever caught in a casino I would be "guilty of criminal trespassing punishable by imprisonment for not more than 1 year and a fine of not more than $1,000, or both."

John will be proud and I can't wait to get home and tell him I've signed out.

NINE

✦

This was it, I said to myself. If I go back to gambling I will be arrested.

At the time I thought the worst was behind me and I was on the way to a "normal" life. I couldn't have been more wrong. My problems were about to get a whole lot worse.

The semi-self-imposed ban on gambling turned me into a maniac. The urge to gamble was as strong as ever but because I had signed out, I was agitated and angry all the time and I took it out on John. What started out as irritation turned into anger and the anger into rage. We had some horrendous knock-down-drag-out fights. I screamed at him, he screamed back, and once I even pushed him down the stairs. I was an out-of-control maniac. I blamed him for everything, particularly the situation I was in having signed out. I wasn't gambling so I suppose it was like a withdrawal I couldn't handle.

I had perfected the art of blaming others for my problem and for my losses. If the nuns at school hadn't made me feel useless, if my father had shown me some love...if John only...

It was easier to blame him than blame myself and I was dishing out enough blame to last a lifetime.

For a while we hardly spoke to each other in anything but a shout.

"Look at yourself. You're falling apart just because you're not playing the stupid..."

"Oh, don't you play the high and mighty with me!"

"This is ridiculous!"

"You want a divorce, is that it? Well I know how to make that happen."

I didn't follow through on the threat but I made sure he knew how angry I was. I was angry at him, at me, at my family, at the world. I was absolutely impossible to live with. Why he didn't leave on the spot, I'll never know. He did, however, take off on long hunting trips, motivated at least in part by the need to get away from me.

On one particular trip he wasn't gone a few hours before I was back at the MGM. It was a Friday night so I figured the casino would be so crowded I could slip in unnoticed. I was both excited and scared. I knew I was taking a big risk, but I was reasonably sure I could get away with it. The excitement brought on by the danger made my pulse race even more than it usually did when I was playing.

I played conservatively so as not to draw attention and I made sure to play where there was a crowd. I was there all evening. No one seemed to notice and it made me feel good to let out some of my anger.

The next day John called and asked what was going on.

"Nothing," I said.

"Nothing really?"

"That's what I said."

"I don't know if I can trust you."

"Well, that's your problem."

After having no difficulty my first time back, I became more daring and started going every time I could find a babysitter—and they weren't hard to find.

One night before John was going to be heading out on a hunting trip, he grilled me like I was a suspect in some terrorist plot.

"You're going to head right back aren't you? Straight to the MGM as soon as my truck backs out of the driveway."

"What difference does it make what I say anyway? You never believe me."

"Should I?"

"I don't know, John, should you?"

"That's up to you. Are you going back to gambling?"

"No. Believe me?"

"I don't know anymore."

"Maybe you should hire Kojack. He'll figure it out."

"Maybe you should start telling the truth for a change."

"Go shoot a rabbit."

The next night while John was in the UP hunting I went straight to the MGM and found a machine to my liking. Soon I became annoyed by a well-dressed woman I had never seen before pacing back and forth near me. Finally she sat down at the machine to my right and stared at it like it was a contraption from another planet. I had seen the bewildered look of a first-time player before.

She looked over at me as if she wanted to cheat off of my test answers in a high school math test. "You look like you know what you're doing here," she said.

"Well, I've done it a few times before if that's what you mean."

"I thought I'd give it a try."

I didn't think anything about giving her a few instructions although one of the nice things about playing slots is that they're really simple to operate. It's not like playing craps or some of the other games where it's all strategy and mental gymnastics.

"Well, you just slide your coins into the slot there," I said pointing to the right place. "You're playing a multiple-line machine and that means that they reward play on more than one line."

She looked at me like I was talking a foreign language.

"That is, one coin pays on line one, two coins on line two, three coins on line three, and so forth. Every time you put in a coin the line will light up. Just make sure you wait for the lines to light before you play. The window up there will show you how many credits you have, then hit the "spin reels" button and wait for your money to fall into the hopper. That's about it really."

"Thanks. I'll give it a try."

When she started playing, I gave her a few more tips, but didn't think much more about her until I saw her there again the next night. I began to think she wasn't there for the playing, she was there for the watching, and the person she was watching was me. I decided to test this by moving to another machine on another aisle. There she was again. One more move and she still followed.

John was having me followed. I was furious. I'll admit I wasn't thinking clearly at all at the time, but just the thought of my husband doing that to me made my blood boil. I was so angry at him that I vowed to get even. I'd gamble every night while he was gone that week.

About four days later, John called.   I could tell he'd been drinking.

"Where are you?" he asked.

"Where are you? I responded.

"Escanaba."

That was a good-sized town but not exactly near where he was supposed to be hunting.   "Don't you have to get up early in the morning to chase after animals?"

He raised his voice.   "What difference does it make where I am? Where the hell are you?"

"Since you hired a detective to follow me, you tell me.   Where am I now?"

"What are you talking about?"

"Don't play stupid.   If you were going to hire a detective, you should have hired a better one.   I spotted her in a minute."

"Really?"

"Really."

"So you are at the casino?"

"Ask her."

"I'm asking you."

"You might as well get you money's worth.   How much did she cost anyway?"

"Don't tell me you're concerned about wasting money!"

I slammed the phone down and headed straight to the MGM. John must have called the detective because I didn't see her there for the rest of the week, but I sure as heck was.

By the time John got home, I had calmed down some and promised yet again I'd stop going to the casino.   But, of course that was just another lie in an ever-expanding string of them.

"You signed out! Don't you know you're going to get arrested?"

"Tell me you didn't get a deer.   We don't have room in the fridge."

John and I were now fighting day and night.   On more than one occasion I told him I had enough of his accusations.   One night as I was backing out of the garage he threw a ten-pound sack of potatoes at my SUV.   They landed on the roof and with every turn I lost a couple of more as they bounced along the street. I went straight to the MGM, potato sack and all.

I learned later that John called the Gaming Board that night and told them I was at the MGM Grand at that moment and that I needed to be removed. He even gave them the make of my SUV, the plate number, and a description of what I was wearing. He did this for several nights, but no one from the casino ever approached me, even though according to the Disassociated Persons List I had signed, they weren't supposed to allow me in there. They had my picture. They had my fingerprints. They had John's description of my clothing. They probably have more security cameras than the CIA. Still, they did nothing. As long as I was there dropping money into the slots and getting little in return, they stayed away from me like I had swine flu.

To pay for all of this I would usually get money from our Credit Union savings or checking accounts. Sometimes I would stop at an ATM machine before going to the casino. Then one evening I ran out of money and decided to try their ATM machine. If nothing else, this should have alerted them immediately that I was illegally in their casino, but nothing happened. As time went by, I became more daring and used their ATMs whenever I needed to.

About a year went by after signing out on the Disassociated Persons List and one evening I had maxed out my credit card for the daily cash amount allowed, so I took the chance and used the phone they had next to the ATM's. This phone would override the cardholder's agreement and check to see if you were good for the money. I'm not sure exactly how it worked, but after I pushed some buttons on the phone and told them how much I needed they approved me and I proceeded to the cashier's cage. The cashier already had the document at the cage, so all I had to do was show my driver's license and sign the back of the check (made payable to MGM Casino) and the teller handed over the cash.

Since the casino was so considerate to make playing there easy, I began to use this money-getting service regularly.

"Hi, Barbara, here's your money. Have a good day."

"Nice to see you again, Barbara. Here's your money. Good luck."

In time I realized that between MGM and the credit card company I was paying around $60 for this transaction. So I tried cashing a personal check. The same thing happened, except there were no charges either from the casino or the credit union.

I played consistently despite the fact that the Disassociated Persons List specifically states that "A casino licensee shall not extend credit, or offer check cashing privileges" to anyone on the list and that "if a casino licensee identifies a person on the premises of the casino, the licensee shall immediately notify the board, a representative of the board, or a representative of the department of state police who is on the premises of the casino." After they confirm that the person has signed the list the casino must: "(a) Immediately remove the individual from the premises. (b) Report the incident to the prosecutor for the county in which the casino is located." It also says, "A casino licensee who violates this act is subject to disciplinary action by the board."

There was absolutely no possibility that the casino didn't know I was there gambling regularly. They knew I was there, they knew I was playing, they knew I was losing. So much for the Disassociated Persons List and the law.

By now I was gambling every day and John was quickly losing whatever little sliver of patience he had left.

One night he said, "I can't compete with the machines anymore. I'm filing for divorce."

The thought of living on my own again terrified me. So did the thought of another divorce proceeding.

I responded by doing what I so often did—I ran away. I jumped in my car and crying all the way, drove to Hines Park. I found a place to park where I couldn't be seen from the road or the parking lot, turned off the car, took out the bottle of prescription Vicodin pain killers, and began swallowing a couple every two minutes.

I felt like there was a huge weight pinning me down, that I was overwhelmed by all sorts of conflicting emotions. I felt tremendous guilt for putting John and my family through so much. I felt ashamed. I felt irrational anger towards John because he saw through my lies. I was depressed because I was trapped in a hopeless and helpless situation. I was in pain. It was all so confusing because I didn't know how to cope other than to escape, and suicide is the ultimate escape.

I put my head back on my headrest. Within a few minutes I

became drowsy and my skin felt like it was getting cold and clammy. My heart rate was slowing down and I was nauseous.

I picked up my cell phone and called Denise. "I just want to tell you that I love you?"

"I know that," she said. "What's wrong?"

"Because you never judged me."

"Real friends don't do that."

"You're the best friend I ever had. Will ever have."

She could tell that I was in a very emotional state by my hysterical sobbing and shaky voice.

"Where are you?"

"I can't take the shame anymore. I can't. I just can't. Everything that I've done to everybody…"

"You're not doing anything stupid, are you?"

"I just want you to know that I really love you."

"I know, you've told me. What are you doing? Are you taking something?"

"You've always been there for me."

"And I am now. Where are you?"

"Someplace."

"Are you at home? I'll come over."

"No."

"No, you're not at home, or no, you don't want me to come over?"

I was crying so hard by then that all I could choke out was "I love you," and hung up.

Within seconds the phone was ringing. Denise was calling back but I didn't answer. I locked the doors and tried to take long deep breaths. Like everyone else I guess, I'd wondered how it would end for me, but I never envisioned this—alone in a car, so depressed and full of regret. It wasn't supposed to be like this.

I know taking your own life is probably the most selfish thing in the world, but the feeling that I couldn't cope with my problems was so strong that it was the only thing in my mind.

In my head I wrote a letter to John that I know will never be sent.

I'm tired. I'm tired of all the lies. I'm tired of being who I am. I'm tired of life.

The phone rang and rang while I continued to take the pills and tried to finish the letter. Soon I was in such an awful state that all I wanted to do was just close my eyes and have it all go away. No more pain or shame and no one able to judge me anymore.

But after a while I picked up the phone again.

"You've got to tell me where you are. Let me come over and we'll talk this through. I won't stop you if that's what you really want, but let's talk about it. Where are you? Right now, where are you?"

"I'm just so sorry I got you involved with this."

"That doesn't matter. Tell me where you are."

"I never should have."

"Barbara, where are you?"

"You're the only one who stayed by me without judging me. The only one."

"I'm here for you now. I've always been, but you can't do this to yourself. Think of Mindy, and Cathy, and John. Think of me. If nothing else think of what you're doing to me. I'll never be able to live with myself if you go through with this. Do you really want to do that to me? I don't think you do."

"I know I'm to blame for everything I've put everybody through and I hate myself for it and I can't live with that."

"You're not thinking straight that's all. You can get through this. We can get through this. Let me help. Please. For me if for nobody else."

"It's too late for that."

"So you want to take the easy way out and let everybody else who cares about you suffer because of your selfishness."

I knew she was right but I didn't say anything for a long time. I guess my pause said it all. 'What's going to happen to the girls without you? And John? He's going to have to go through the rest of his life in agony because he'll think it was his fault. Your mom, father, brothers and sisters, you'll be punishing them, too. The only one you won't punish is you. You won't have to worry about anything. Everybody else who loves you will."

"It's the only way out I know," I said and pressed "end" on my cell phone.

Maybe another half hour or so of constant unanswered cell phone ringing passed and I was growing drowsier by the minute. The sleepier

I got, the more I felt sorry for myself. "I'm so ashamed," was all I could think about. It's driven me to lie, to commit illegal acts, and now to this. I had filled my life with superficial promises that lacked purpose and substance. I had created a life based on lies and, yet, I think I realized that everything that Denise had said was right. I was being a coward.

Then I answered the phone again. I don't know why. It would be easy to say it was because deep down I really wanted Denise to ride to my rescue, but I don't know that's true. At least it didn't seem that way. When I arrived at the park I had every intention of ending my pain then and there, but what Denise had said made sense, too. I was so disoriented I'm not sure I knew what I was doing.

Now she was also crying and I could tell how much I was hurting her.

"Please, please, please tell me where you are?"

"I don't know exactly. I'm in a park."

"What park? Where?"

By this time I was so confused and drowsy I couldn't concentrate enough to remember where I had driven. "A park, back behind the trees."

"A park. By your house? The park near where you live?"

"I guess so."

I don't know how long it was—probably not more than five minutes—before Denise showed up with her older daughter so that she could drive my car.

Denise knocked on my window. "Open up, Barbara. Open up."

As soon as I did she grabbed the remainder of the pills. "Come on, let me help you out of here." She and her daughter put their arms around me and led me behind a little nearby shed.

"Stick your finger down your throat and make yourself throw up. You've got to get rid of those pills. Go ahead, try."

After a few attempts I finally managed to get my finger down far enough. I threw up several times, before they took me back to Denise's house. I threw up a few more times in her toilet, and then they helped me to take of my clothes and put me into a cold shower. All the while I was in a dull daze, saying little but doing everything Denise asked through cloudy eyes.

I sprawled on her bed and she sat with me for hours to make sure

I was okay. Eventually I fell asleep and she slept next to me through the night. When I woke in the morning I told her how sorry I was and we had a long conversation about true and unconditional love as best friends.

I was humiliated by what I had put her through. It wasn't right, of course, but neither was what I had done to my family

"I was really scared, Barbara," she said. "I thought I was going to lose you, lose my best friend. I don't know what I would have done. You scared the crap out of me."

"I know," I said.

"I want us to grow old together as friends and let God decide when it's our time."

She told me she had called John and told him I was all right and would be staying the night with her. She would call him if anything happened.

No one could ask for a better friend. She can be a little rough on the outside, a little tomboyish country girl. She loves to play and watch sports and can be about as competitive as they come. There weren't many men around who dared take her on in pool. But underneath her rough exterior is a heart of gold.

I've asked myself many times since that night whether I would have gone all the way had she not been there and the answer is I think I would have.

I was pretty groggy all day, most of which was spent talking to Denise. But there was never any "you're a bad person" talk. She was playing the role of friend not judge and jury.

Ever since they opened the casinos in Detroit, the number of suicides had risen significantly. I certainly wasn't the first compulsive gambler who decided it was the best way out of a personal hell. In fact, by law, the Michigan lottery has to contribute $1 million dollars a year to a compulsive gambling fund and the three Detroit casinos, another $2 million. The idea was to offer counseling to those who needed it, but of course, the gambler has to acknowledge the problem first.

In the afternoon I called John.

"I want to come home, John."

"I'm not so sure that's a good idea."

"I know you know what happened last night and I just..."

"I've already seen an attorney and he's drawn up the papers. They're ready to sign as soon as I can get to his office."

"I need to talk to you."

"I'm not sure what good it will do. We've been all through this I don't know how many times. Despite what you've said, you're not willing to acknowledge and deal with your problem."

"I am now."

After a long pause, "Okay. I'll be here."

When I got to the house he was in the garage waiting for me. It was probably the most awkward moment of my life. He didn't say anything as I approached and I didn't know how to handle the situation. I certainly didn't know what to say. I didn't know what I could say. For that matter, I really didn't know how I felt about things. I knew my life was falling apart in front of me and I didn't know how to pick up the pieces.

After some moments with both of us standing silently in the garage, I finally told him about everything that had happened the night before. I told him how desperate I was, how I felt so lost and ashamed.

He was sympathetic but very guarded. "I've heard this before Barbara. I've heard how sorry you are but it never lasts. I don't doubt that you mean it when you say it, but you go right back to your old ways. I can't live with you being like that."

"I'd like another chance."

"How many have you already had?"

"I know, but right now I need your support more than ever. I have a CAT scan next week. I have a nodule on my lung that's growing. The doctor's very worried and I'm scared out of my mind."

He looked at me like he was saying, "Is this another one of your bullshit stories?" It was. I may not have been a very good wife or mother at that point but I was one hell of a good liar and wasn't going to pass up the opportunity to play the sympathy card.

"You know about the nodule from past scans," I said. "Well now it's growing."

"When's the appointment for the scan?"

"Wednesday," I said. That was the truth. I had a routine scan scheduled for then but there never was a suggestion that the nodule was growing.

"If you come back, you can't go to the casinos. Not even once. If you do, I'm going ahead with the divorce."

"I came close enough to dying last night. I think I've learned a lesson."

I could see he was skeptical about the story but he took a deep breath and said, "All right, I'll give it one more try."

That Wednesday he drove me to the CAT scan and I think that's when he finally believed my story. He called the attorney and told him he'd hold off on signing the papers.

"My attorney told me that was a mistake," John said. "He said it was only going to get worse."

"Attorneys don't always know everything," I assured him.

"Please don't make him right."

"I won't."

Within a week I was gambling again. John figured it out right away. This time he didn't say much. What he did was close the bank accounts to which I had access and pretty much took my name off of everything he could. His business was doing better than we had ever expected so there was a considerable amount of money coming in. But he was so busy keeping up with the demands of the work, putting on employees, negotiating new contracts, and the like that he didn't always have time to pay attention to every little financial detail. The simple fact is that neither of us immediately realized that I was spending it even faster than he was making it.

I still had credit cards in my name although I was fast maxing them out. If I wasn't putting every penny I could get my hands on into the machines, I was buying things for my daughter in a futile effort to make up for the guilt I was feeling.

I had turned into a frenetic, out-of-control, constantly lying, demon. John and I were basically living separate lives. We talked little, avoided each other when we could, and fought when we couldn't. Sometimes he'd want to take Cathy with him on his trips to the UP and I'd always pick a fight so I didn't have to go. We both knew I'd rather go gambling than hunting. Actually, I'd rather go gambling than just about anyplace else.

One Saturday afternoon shortly before Christmas, John was at work and Cathy was staying the night at a friend's house. I decided to head to the MGM with the idea that if John called I'd tell him I was Christmas shopping. This time though…

Mid-December, 2006, Detroit, Michigan

Waiting for the mailman every day is like waiting for news on the outcome of your brain operation. I am a nervous wreck. I want the letter to come. I don't want the letter to come.

I know I should tell John but I keep convincing myself it is the holiday season and I don't want to spoil it for him.

I keep myself busy with shopping and baking.

I anxiously wait for the mail. I pray to God the casino letter doesn't come on a Saturday when there is a chance John will get to it before I do.

I take Cathy to the toy store, stop for groceries, come home, check the mail.

I go out for more wrapping paper, fill up the gas tank, come home, check the mail.

I bake, wrap, check the mail.

The tension is wearing me down like sandpaper on soft wood.

I check the mail. Nothing.

Christmas Eve, 2006, Detroit, Michigan

Everything is fuzzy as if in a dream. I feel like I am outside looking in at myself through dirty glass. I am going through the motions of a merry Christmas that is anything but. The knot in my stomach and the dryness in my throat stop me from eating much of the dinner or the Christmas cookies I usually devour. Everyone notices.

"Just a little indigestion," I say as the latest in a long line of lies.

We are at my mother-in-law's for a traditional Polish Christmas Eve feast just as we have been for many Christmases past.

Cathy no longer believes in Santa Claus but we go through the motions of pretending. I've gotten good at pretending, at hiding, at avoiding. Truth and lies, real and unreal, fact and fiction. I'm not sure I know the difference anymore.

We go into the living room after dinner. There must be laughter and joy but I don't notice. I am overwhelmed by guilt and unrelenting tension. The only way to break it is to tell John, but I can't tell John.

I am on the brink. I could explode any minute.

John is trading fishing stories with his stepdad. They are laughing. I force a smile which must look as phony as a million dollar payout.

During a lull in the laughter, I think John asks, "Where are the gift cards?" but it is as if he is in another place.

"What?"

I am sure everyone can tell there is something wrong with me but no one says anything. Have I gotten that good at pretending?

"The gift cards?"

"Oh, in my purse I think."

A soft Silent Night, Holy Night *comes from someplace. Maybe the radio. "Silent night, holy night, all is calm, all is bright…"*

"Mind telling me where that is? Your purse."

"Uh, upstairs on the bed."

John goes upstairs to look for the cards for the older nieces and nephews.

He is gone for longer than it should take to find the cards but I think nothing of it. When he comes down the stairs, though I know there is something seriously wrong. He is never hard for me to read.

He hands out the cards. I am so nervous, I can hardly stand to say our good byes.

On the way home he is quiet but doesn't say what is wrong. I don't ask. I don't want to know.

At home we unpack gifts and tell Cathy to go to bed so we can put her presents under the tree.

John hands me a receipt from the MGM Grand, dated December 6.

Christmas Day, 2006, Detroit, Michigan

John knows everything. I am glad it is out but it does little to relieve the tension and nothing to relieve the shame and guilt.

I feel like I have lost the battle, not just with gambling, but the battle with life itself.

I don't know why he is still with me. If the shoe were on the other foot, I think I would have run off a long time ago. But then that is what I do. I run to avoid.

Throughout the day I try to keep the communications open, but it appears he has no fight left in him.

He is quiet, even morose when Cathy is not around but he doesn't confront me. There is no big argument, no angry raised-voice scene, no acknowledgement. I almost wish there would be.

It looks like Christmas, and with the turkey in the oven it smells that way, but it certainly doesn't feel that way. There is tension in every pause, veiled anger in every word.

Cathy acts thrilled with her presents but I know she can tell there is something wrong between Mommy and Daddy and that makes me very, very, sad. Isn't it bad enough what I have done to John and myself, without having to spoil the joy of a child?

All day I am close to tears, but fight them back for her sake.

I know I have spoiled the lives of everyone I love and I hate myself for that.

I can't help painting pictures in my mind: After the holidays, John packing and leaving. A custody hearing before the judge. An empty house. I am not in any of the pictures. I have disappeared.

TEN

✦

After my arrest at the MGM, John and I went together to see the criminal lawyer who was recommended to us with the idea that he may be able to work out a plea deal. We had with us the letter from the State of Michigan Department of State Police, saying there was a warrant out for my arrest.

So now I wasn't just an addicted gambler, an irresponsible wife, mother, and daughter, but a criminal as well.

It was possible under the law that I could be sentenced to up to a year in prison. No matter how hard I tried, I couldn't stop thinking about it. My mind ran amuck as I conjured up images remembered from movies or television shows I had seen. Women crammed into little cells, women fighting women, women having sex with other women, women being mistreated by sadistic male guards. I already have enough mental scars and I don't need any physical ones. Maybe it wouldn't have been like this but I couldn't stop my mind from imagining the worst and it scared the daylights out of me.

I was so nervous when we went to see the attorney I could hardly steady my legs under me. What if he said the best deal we could hope for was something less than the full year? Maybe nine months. Maybe six.

The attorney's fee was $1,500 which John paid up front, but it wasn't easy for him, because I had gone through so much of our money that we were in a very tight financial situation. Exactly how tight I didn't know because I never kept track of the money I had dumped into the machines. If an ATM would give me money, I spent it; if a credit card had room on it, I used it.

For years John had been working his tail off so that we would have financial security. Neither one of us had grown up in situations where money wasn't an issue, but John had put us in that position before I ruined it. I'm not sure exactly how much money I had lost gambling but I don't think $600,000 is an exaggeration. John thinks it was closer to $700,000. At any rate, add to that interest on the credit card balances and the figure gets ridiculous. The thought that I could have wasted close to $1 million dollars is positively disgusting.

It's not surprising that we were on the verge of bankruptcy. Our savings were gone, the bills were piling up, and on top of everything else the economy in Michigan was in a near death spiral that was beginning to have a terrible effect on John's business. We were both worried sick that we were going to have to come up with even more money to deal with the arrest warrant.

The lawyer asked us a bunch of questions and then said that he knew the prosecuting attorney and would try to work out a deal.

"What kind of a deal?" I asked.

"If all goes well, perhaps only probation."

"And if it doesn't go well."

"We'll cross that bridge if and when we come to it."

I left his office feeling a little better, but certainly not confident. I'd lay awake at night thinking about things like whether in prison I'd have an upper bunk or a lower one, whether I'd have to wear an orange coverall, whether I'd be taken away in handcuffs.

We had to go to court a couple of times, but in the end, the attorneys did work out a deal. I was put on probation for a period of one year and assessed $600 in fines and costs. We were in such bad shape that we couldn't come up with that so they let me set up payments of $70 a month which I was to pay at my monthly meetings with my probation officer. The conditions of the probation were that I would have no contact with any casino, would be screened for gambling addiction by the Michigan Department of Community Health, and would have no further contact with the criminal justice system. I also had to see a counselor for gambling addiction treatment.

Linda was maybe the nicest person I had ever met. She was a counselor who understood what I had been going through as a gambling addict. Still, it wasn't easy to talk about it and often I ended our sessions in tears.

I met her regularly in her office. She was neat, organized, friendly, and very professional. She was always trying to get me to see the good in everything and everyone but I couldn't shake the horrible guilt I felt over the financial stress I had put on John.

I was both a pathological liar and a pathological gambler so addicted that until I was arrested, I couldn't break the cycle.

I learned a lot in my counseling sessions. I learned that slot machines and video poker (which I didn't play) are considered the "crack cocaine" of gambling probably because they offer immediate gratification.

I know now that while some women engage in action gambling, most of us are attracted to what they call escape or luck gambling such as Bingo or slots. We gamble more to escape than to engage. Depression often accompanies us but whether the depression brought on the gambling or vice versa I don't know. All I know is the excitement of playing brought some relief.

Most woman become problem gamblers as a result of loneliness, anxiety, or depression. Women tend to go for slots because they can play them alone and there is little skill involved. Slots create a world where we can exist apart from our unhappiness in broken marriages or difficult family situations.

Women tend to progress toward problem gambling much faster than men. On average the racetrack player or serious card player often take twenty or more years to hit bottom. The average for slot players is two years. We also tend to experience a greater amount of shame and guilt while still playing. I know I certainly did.

"Why me?" I kept asking Linda. "How could I have let the gambling get so out of control?"

"It's a disease," she'd say. "A mental disease, but like most illnesses, it can be overcome. Barbara, I'm going to tell you something very important and I want to make absolutely sure you understand it. Here it is: You are very sick, but it's not your fault. Compulsive gambling is a progressive disorder that typically starts out as frivolous enjoyment and ends up as destructive to both the gambler and the gambler's family. Sound familiar?"

"Yeah."

"Like alcoholism, it's a disease for which there is no known cure, but with help its progress can be arrested. I'm that help, Barbara, but you've got to stay open to that help. You've got to want that help."

She suggested that my relationship to my parents might have had something to do with it. "Perhaps you were always looking for approval from your parents. That could very well have been the trigger." She told me that a high percentage of people who develop gambling problems had lousy childhoods of one sort or another. Well, that may be so, but to use it as an excuse seemed like a giant cop out.

Anyway, whether that's true or not, I couldn't blame anyone but myself. Linda kept telling me I was too hard on myself but that's how I felt.

"I've ruined every dream John's had since he was a kid. How can he possibly ever forgive me? He shouldn't. He can't."

"I think he can and he will if he hasn't already for one simple reason: He's in love with you."

"I don't know why he's stayed."

"That's why."

"I don't deserve it."

"Barbara, you have to forgive yourself and move on. You can't live in the past."

I listened to Linda. I really did, but it wasn't that easy to let go of the past. It haunted me, tormented me, and clung onto me like it was nailed there.

All the while I was seeing her, our financial situation was worsening. The bills were piling up and the interest on all the money I had put on credit cards was skyrocketing. We should have been sailing in secure financial waters, but the reality was, we were sinking.

For the first time in nine years I couldn't go to my daughter's dance nationals because we couldn't afford it. I think this is when reality really rose up and slapped me in the face. I tried to put on a good front to John and Cathy, but I was really devastated.

She had been dancing since she was five and had shown real talent in ballet, jazz, and modern dance. After about three years of lessons, her school began competing in national dance competitions. Each July we would go with her to whichever state was hosting the nationals that year. Cathy always stood out in the solo as well as group competitions. She was that good and so was her school. They were usually the ones to beat for the top prizes.

She also got into runway modeling when she was seven and

competed in local fashion shows, even winning such titles as Junior Miss Michigan, Miss St. Patrick, etc.

It was hard to face the fact that I could no longer go with her to some of these events. It was a hard enough struggle as it was just to get from month to month.

When we finally couldn't avoid it any longer, we went to see a bankruptcy lawyer. He was amazed that it took so long for the MGM to arrest me. As long as I was losing, they let me in, but as soon as I won...

The lawyer's fee was $1,500 which wasn't easy for us to come by but we did manage to file bankruptcy on about $75,000 of our debt. We were, however, able to affirm a few debts in the bankruptcy like the mortgage on our house and a second mortgage on one of the rental properties that we owned.

I continued to see Linda and usually left her office feeling a little better, but by the time I got home, reality set in. I was sick, incredibly anxious, unable to control either my thoughts or actions, and I was unbearably depressed. I was in my private hell, a hell that the nuns never told us about.

I thought that I had hit rock bottom before but I was falling into a state of utter despair and I could see no way out. I felt absolutely useless. I doubt if anyone can understand the feeling without having gone through it. It is not mere sadness. It is a feeling of weight born of shame. It robbed me of the possibility of feeling any pleasure. My energy was low and my motivation to do anything about it was virtually nonexistent. Just getting from day to day was a chore. It is not a condition that can be willed or wished away. You can't just "snap out of it."

I had messed up my life and the life of others. And I was finding it hard to live with that. I had my chances but had ruined everything. I had had enough.

When one night John fell asleep on the couch, I went to the kitchen, got two bottles of water, went up stairs, and found my vial of Percocet.

In my head I finished the letter to John that I know will never be sent.

I'm tired. I'm tired of all the lies. I'm tired of being who I am. I'm tired of life.

I'd like to say I tried, but I guess the painful truth is that I didn't try hard enough. I couldn't stay away from the machines. Couldn't, didn't, I don't know.

I've lost so much—our money, my integrity, your trust. I've lost all that and more and now I'm losing my last grip on life—I'm losing hope. No, I've lost hope, the latest loss in a lifetime filled with loss. It depresses me, makes me mad, fills my every waking moment with guilt, and I can't live with that. I won't live with that. I know what "utter despair" means. It means I've reached the end.

I'm sorry. Sorry about everything.

I leave you with the only thing I have left—my undying love.

The next thing I remember is waking up in the critical care unit of the hospital. I was groggy but truly upset that I was still alive. This time there were no calls to best friends or veiled hopes that I would be saved at the last moment. This was not a call for help; it was an attempt to kill myself.

John and Denise both came to visit but I was incoherent most of the time and have little recall of what was said. I know I didn't say much.

After three days, although I was still semi-incoherent, John was able to convince the hospital to let me go home. I stayed in bed for days, but John remained by my side through it all. He nursed me back to health in spite of everything I did to him.

Now I had really hit the absolute bottom. There was no place else to go except up or out. With John's unqualified support, I chose up. Why couldn't I have done this earlier? So much sorrow and hurt could have been avoided. I can't say why. Maybe it's the old story that before things can get better, they have to get worse—sometimes a lot worse. I know that my addiction didn't stay in one place. It didn't hit a certain stage and then level off. It kept deepening, affecting me physically, mentally, and morally. On all of those levels I kept getting worse until I finally bottomed out.

In a perverse way hitting bottom may have been my salvation. It has enabled me to bounce back up. Of this I am now very sure: Every addicted gambler has a bottom out there to hit. A place where even the hardest of the hardcore finally admit that their lives have become unmanageable. In my case at least, then and only then was I able to begin to put a fulfilling life back together. The urge to gamble was beaten out of me by the arrest, by the hard bottom I hit. Little by little, I began to return to a life as a normal, healthy wife, mother, and daughter. I haven't stepped into a casino since my arrest at the MGM on December 9, 2006, nor will I ever again.

Now I can see that I am truly the luckiest woman in the world. I have a husband whose love for me never wavered. We may have lost almost everything in the world that we had, but never that love. It is a true love that doesn't come with conditions attached.

May 13, 2009, Detroit, Michigan

A letter comes from the Michigan Gaming Control Board in response to a complaint I had filed against the MGM Grand because they had willingly let me gamble there after I had signed up on the Disassociated Persons List. That is, they let me gamble as long as I was losing money, but as soon as I won, they swooped down on me like a vulture on carrion.

I read the letter carefully. It is from a Regulation Officer of the Board. "Your complaint is important to the Board because the complaint often brings to the Board's attentions serious violations of the Michigan Gaming Control & Revenue Act and Administrative Rules."

Well, that's a good start I think. "It is my understanding that the complaint arose from an incident that you claim you were able to gamble and cash checks after you signed up on the Disassociated Persons List. The review and investigation of your patron dispute against MGM Grand Casino has been completed."

At least they've taken my complaint seriously enough to conduct an investigation. "After a meticulous and detailed review, the MGCB investigation reveals the matters you describe were in fact addressed as a result of a situation, very similar to yours, that took place approximately six months after your incidents. The MGM Grand Detroit Casino took corrective actions in a software upgrade to MGM's check cashing system, which substantially increases MGM cashier's ability to detect persons on the Dissociated Persons List."

I show the letter to John. We both have a good laugh.

John says, "They have better surveillance than our homeland security."

The letter continues, "You may wish to contact your own attorney in order to determine whether there are any civil remedies available to you under the circumstances you describe."

ELEVEN

✦

I know I'm not the first person to succumb to temptations and then in hindsight say, "How could I have?" Nevertheless, the question hovers and, I suppose, always will.

I can't swear this is true, but I've heard that more than 40% of casino profits come from known addicted gamblers. I don't doubt it.

In an effort to recover at least some of my losses, we contacted several lawyers. The casino welcomed me to play and took my money in direct violation of the law. Surely there is a case to be made against the casino. Surely there are attorneys who would like to take on the casinos. That's what we thought anyway.

Make of this what you will. Here are three facts:

1. The Attorney General of the State of Michigan is the person responsible for ensuring that the Gaming Commission is properly enforcing the law with regard to the casinos.

2. The current Attorney General has announced his candidacy for Governor of Michigan.

3. John and I have drawn blanks in trying to find an attorney to take our case against the MGM.

As I see it, you can't get a fair shake against the casinos because the influence of casino profits on our political system is nothing less than astounding. Something like $1 million dollars a day is pumped back into the state's coffers from gambling losses and so it seems the politicians are firmly in the pockets of the casinos.

The odds are as stacked against the player as they are on beating the slots. The casinos are just too big, too powerful for a tall, skinny girl from the suburbs to challenge. We spoke with one attorney who said that as he saw it, the Michigan Gaming Control Board is in partnership with the casinos. "It is a joke," he said. "They do very little. Certainly they don't issue fines, they don't even enforce the laws. Jobs with the Board are political plums handed out by politicians in exchange for favors and no court will do anything to disrupt revenue to the state and to the city because simply put, Detroit can't survive without gambling revenue. The economic interests of the state far outweigh the social costs. Money talks."

The attorney tried to bring an action against a casino but he was immediately sanctioned for filing a frivolous action. It is a cozy relationship how the casinos and the government protect each other from lawsuits seeking damages from casino gambling.

So what's the purpose for the Disassociated Persons List if it's not enforced? What's the purpose for the law?

It's pretty much agreed that compulsive gambling is a disease, much like alcoholism or drug addiction. Should casinos be allowed to profit from people's illnesses? Should they take advantage of sick people? I don't think so.

John and I will go on trying to rebuild our lives, but the lesson is clear: When it comes to casino gambling, you can't win.